SCOTT LANG'S
LEADERSHIP
TRAVEL GUIDE

Also by Scott Lang

with Tim Lautzenheiser, Patrick Sheridan, and Jon Gomez

Leadership Success: A holistic approach to developing your student leadership program

DVD and CD-ROM

SCOTT LANG'S
LEADERSHIP
TRAVEL GUIDE

GIA Publications, Inc.
Chicago

Scott Lang's Leadership Travel Guide
Scott Lang
G-7192

Copyright © 2007 GIA Publications, Inc. • www.giamusic.com
7404 S. Mason Ave., Chicago, IL 60638

ISBN: 978-1-57999-687-1
Printed in the United States of America

Dedication...

To my wife Leah, for without her love, support, vision and constant modeling of what a true leader is, this book would not have been possible. The words may be mine, but I am channeling the life you live. You are the embodiment of what I strive to be.

To my son Brayden, who inspires me and reminds me of why we lead. You are my future, my past, and my present. As you grow, may I grow with you – by your side as a friend, behind you as a father and in front of you as a protector.

A special thanks to...

…my family, for supporting me through this process and being my biggest cheerleaders.

…Clayton Ledford, for being a sounding board for all of my ideas, thoughts and ramblings. Your fingerprints are all over this book and my life.

…Dr. Tim Lautzenheiser for his years of service and dedication to creating the leaders of tomorrow. You blazed the trail and changed innumerable lives, including mine.

…Jon Gomez, my friend and brother. You started me on this journey and continue to pace me.

…Janette Phillips, for your meticulous attention to detail during the editing process. You are a writer's best friend and an ego's worst enemy.

…Terry Jolley and Alexis Yatuzis-Derryberry, for pushing me off the cliff and being there to catch me.

…Alec Harris of GIA Publications, for believing in me when there was nothing to believe in.

…Fran Kick, for being a scholar, leader, mentor and friend.

… Lance Britt and the West Johnston High School Band, for being my inaugural voyagers, explorers, and valued supporters.

…my many friends from the road. You trusted me with your most valued resource, your students. I can only hope that your trust was rewarded and that I have done half as much for you as you have done for me.

For my brother Todd...

CONTENTS

INTRODUCTION
My Tour, Bob As My Guide

"love to travel, but hate to arrive"

Albert Einstein

ABOUT THIS TRAVEL GUIDE

This book was designed to help facilitate a collaborative process between student leaders and program directors. While each can utilize these materials in an individual manner, I believe that it will be more beneficial when used in a collaborative group setting. Some activities are geared more toward the director, some are focused more on the students, and others are a perfect marriage between the two. Regardless of how they are structured, each chapter and activity is designed to benefit everyone involved in the process. Drawing upon fifteen years' experience in the classroom and as a leadership facilitator, I have tried to provide a highly flexible, creative and engaging leadership training experience.

I believe that leadership training is a journey and not a destination; hence the theme of this book. Throughout this book, you will have the opportunity to stop your travel and spend some time in places you deem appropriate, returning to the journey when everyone is ready. Furthermore, you can choose to travel according to my itinerary (sequential order) or visit the various locations (chapters) as you see fit. The decision is yours!

When used in sequential order, the travel guide starts by providing you with an opportunity to sit back and dream big with *Finding Your Compass*. The dream facilitation activities in this section will help you sort through all of those travel brochures (ideas and thoughts other people have on what your leadership journey should look like), pick a destination and chart a course to keep. This is a time to think "big picture" and plan for the future. Try not to be limited in your thinking and be willing to be open to the ideas of others who are sharing in your trip experience.

The next section, ***Before You Travel: The Basics***, examines the values and behaviors commonly associated with the journey of student leadership. This is a chance before you begin your trip to agree on some ground rules for the group. This unit will lead you through a series of thought provoking questions and thematic activities to help facilitate the process of creating a clear and concise set of beliefs for everyone to abide by while on our leadership adventure.

Traveling Alone: The Leader Within will help you find and identify your core values as they relate to being a leader. It is my belief that most adults, much less students, cannot clearly identify their core beliefs when it comes to leadership. On the surface, we often adopt the leadership values espoused by our families, friends, religion and even pop culture. This unit will challenge you to look within and find your authentic leadership beliefs and begin to develop a comprehensive approach to leadership based on your views.

Since you are not on this leadership journey alone, ***Traveling With A Group: Leading Throughout***, will show how everyone's individual values can fit with those of the group. This unit will attempt to bring everyone's leadership style to the forefront, see what values are common to the entire group and what individual values may need to be placed on the shelf for use in another trip. This unit will also work to ensure that each participant is placed in a position where their skills match their responsibilities.

The ***Conclusion*** of the book and the ***Appendix*** provide for some brief thoughts, ideas, and scenarios which can fill some down time or just get the creative juices flowing.

Start your journey from the beginning, middle, or end. Travel with a specific itinerary or travel freely; on your time, in your way. Work alone, as a small group or as a leadership team. Complete the activities or just use them as an opportunity to ignite a group discussion. How and when you use this book should be a reflection of your individuality and leadership style. This is your journey. You should proceed in a manner that reflects your individuality as a person and uniqueness as a group.

As you will soon discover, I do not believe that there is ONE way to lead, and I am most certain that there is no ONE way to teach it.

This book is designed to help you and your organization find a leadership style and a set of values that is authentic to you and the culture of your group. Take your time and let your journey take you where it should, not where you *want*. As an individual or leader, be flexible, patient and willing to listen to others. Then and only then will you find your authentic leadership style.

To help further clarify some of the activities and materials contained within this book I am including an **icon index**. This visual road map will help you get the most out of the book by highlighting important points, giving you points to ponder and opportunities to reflect on the distance you have traveled and the sights you have seen.

Please drop me a line and let me know what you think or share an idea for the next book. I am always looking for help from my friends. Good luck on your journey. Travel safe and be sure to send me pictures from your destinations!

ICON LEGEND

The icons below are meant to serve as a legend to this travel guide. These icons will serve as a visual cue and will allow you to quickly assess what the item is and how it should be used. This should allow you to be more efficient and effective as you move through the materials.

Travel Advisory

This is a warning to stop and think before proceeding. The statements made or questions posed are worth your consideration, contemplation, and discussion.

Post Card

This is something that requires you to document your thoughts for future discussion and or review. Use the space provided to begin the writing process and use additional space or paper where needed.

Picture Moment

Stop and take a mental picture here as it represents a thought or idea you will want to remember later on. Highlight it or respond to it in the margins of the book if you have something to add to the thought.

Travelogue

A space to journal your thoughts, ideas and questions from recent pages. Use this space not to regurgitate what you have learned but to expound on it and apply it to your group and your life.

Travel Tip

A tip from a frequent flier in the leadership world.

Car Game

These are meant as conversations to pass the time when there is a down moment. You can do it in small or large groups.

Packing List

Things to think about as you pack and unpack from your current location. This should serve as an opportunity to reflect at the end of each chapter. You can do this in writing or as a discussion piece.

Activity

A physical and interactive moment that reinforces the materials presented earlier in the chapter.

PASSPORT CHECK

PASSPORT TO A ROAD LESS TRAVELED

NAME

_____

☐ *Introduction*

☐ *Chapter One*

☐ *Chapter Two*

☐ *Chapter Three*

☐ *Chapter Four*

Be sure to take lots of notes during this journey. Even the best memories can't capture each and every nuance of a trip. Scribble in the margins, doodle on the cover, add your own ideas, and use the travelogues at the end of each chapter to reflect on your thoughts and review your progress and growth. This will also allow you to revisit your destinations and your thoughts in the days, weeks, and years to come.

My maiden voyage...

Fifteen years as a classroom teacher and program director have provided me with numerous opportunities for laughter, learning and leading. My experiences in developing student leaders have, if nothing else, forced me to look within and address my own strengths and shortcomings. Putting in print what I believe to be of importance has proven to be the ultimate barometer of personal truth and individual integrity. Translating these beliefs into action has challenged me to participate in the process of self-improvement along with my students. Just like you, some of my days are filled with more success than others. Believe it or not, the genesis of my path was born out of the desire to instill leadership qualities not in myself, but in my students. My growth has just been an unexpected benefit.

> **PICTURE MOMENT**
>
> *My growth has just been an unexpected benefit.*

As I evolved personally and professionally from a young and inexperienced teacher to where I am today, I began to search for greater meaning in my teaching, something more than trophies and accolades for a job well done. Sure, the positive affirmations from parents, colleagues and adjudicators felt good, but as my days on the podium grew in number, the accolades became less meaningful to me. As my time in the classroom grew, so did the void once filled by approval. The accolade junkie in me began to fade away and I was caught in search of my next professional "fix."   I began to wonder, was I changing? What was changing? Did my students or I cause this change?

POSTCARD

What is your fix? What keeps you going?

How has it changed since you began this activity?

I still loved teaching, but as I approached various performance venues and festivals, I lacked the awe and wonder that accompanied these events earlier in my career. I do not mean to trivialize past successes or failures as they are an important part of both my and the program's evolutionary process. As I grew, I just felt that I needed to find other challenges – something in addition to just preparing for performances and meeting standards. So I began my search.

CAR GAME

Does performing still have the same awe and wonder for you as when you started high school (or started teaching)?

How has it changed?

How have you changed?

I started by looking at my students through a more holistic lens and wondered what, if anything, I was doing to prepare them for success, and not just in my curricula, but also in life. This search led me to seek a greater sense of purpose than could be achieved through performance alone. I sought something that would stand the test of time and truly serve students in all facets of their lives. This is what started me down the path of student leadership: a sense of greater purpose, not only for my students but for myself as well.

So how did the process begin for me? Who showed me that leadership development would not only lead to better performers but more importantly, better people? His name was Stephen Peterson, a successful predecessor of mine and current Director of Bands at Ithaca College.

Years ago, while he was in town for a holiday break visiting his family, I asked him to work with my (his former) ensemble. After spending several hours on the podium with them he and I spent some time reflecting. He was very complimentary of the group and spoke highly of their

TRAVEL ADVISORY

How much of your class/program is designed to inspire student ownership?

How much ownership do the students take in the program?

How can this be increased?

performance skills. I shared with him my concern that they weren't playing to their fullest ability and asked him, "What can I do to get them to give me that last ten percent?" Since I was familiar with his past recordings and performances (which include a performance at several preeminent music events including The Midwest Clinic), I could see that he had been able to successfully get students to that level and beyond. He smiled and said in a knowing voice, "Nothing…only they can take the last step. What are you doing to teach that?"

This was the wake-up call I was looking for. He had shown me a new way to approach my teaching and given me a new canvas on which to paint. Almost immediately, I began planning. I started reading everything I could get my hands on. I started meeting more regularly with my student leaders. I revamped my leadership selection process and required student leaders to, among other things, attend workshops and read leadership materials. Finally, I developed my own student leadership retreat and began training students myself. As I look back now, most of what I taught in those early years involved someone else's thoughts and ideas; I just presented them. Even still, this process allowed me the opportunity to define who I was as an educator and what I believed. This was a special time for me and my students in which the awe and wonder of teaching and learning was re-energized by this new content area. It is my hope that this book will serve the same purpose for you and your leadership team.

 Fast-forward fifteen years...

Jon Gomez, a good friend and colleague, called me and said he had just come from a restaurant where he was seated next to a group of my former students. He said nothing to them, nor did they recognize him as someone they knew. Seeing this as a golden opportunity to be a fly on the wall, he sat and listened attentively as they regaled in stories and memories from the past. He said it was touching to hear the students speak so highly of their band experience.

Curious to hear their perspectives, I asked my colleague what he had overheard. Without missing a beat he responded, "They spoke of the character you instilled and the life lessons they learned." He stated that the students said nothing of their performance experiences, which included concerts with the Canadian Brass, the President of the United States, and the Tournament of Roses Parade. Given the prominence of these events, I was surprised not to hear what I considered to be milestone events mentioned as a part of the conversation. Instead of reliving their performances, they celebrated and remembered how the program placed personal integrity at a premium. They also spoke of how our band credos "Discipline Before Instruction, Behavior Before Performance" and "We Are Better Only If We Work Harder" helped shaped their lives, both then and now.

PICTURE MOMENT

They also spoke of how our band credos "Discipline Before Instruction, Behavior Before Performance" and "We Are Better Only If We Work Harder" helped shaped their lives, both then and now.

TRAVEL ADVISORY

Fifteen years from now, what will people remember about their experiences?

What will they say about you?

Needless to say, as I hung up the phone, I was deeply affected by what I had heard. As I began to wonder more about the students, I began to do the math and deduced that these students were from that original leadership group I had started some fifteen years ago. It was nice to know that in some small way, I had helped to prepare them for life both inside and outside of the concert hall.

Can you achieve success without investing in the development of character? Absolutely! Will the members of your group have a positive educational experience? Quite possibly. Will they not only remember their experiences, but also draw from them in search of continued success after high school? Not likely. A curriculum alone lasts just as long as it serves your needs. Character serves you

PICTURE MOMENT

Teach the musician and you teach to the moment. Teach the child and you teach to the future.

for life and provides the foundation for learning all curricula. Teach the musician and you teach to the moment, teach the child and you teach to the future.

What are you doing to ensure that the members of your section/group are willing to give that last ten percent? What are you doing to ensure their success outside of the band room and after high school? How long will what you taught them be of value? These are the questions that started my journey, so it only seems fitting that they start yours.

And so we begin…

Bob and Me

The lesson of personal sacrifice and unyielding demands for excellence was one I learned in high school. Like a forgotten memory, the lesson would not reveal itself to me and prove meaningful until much later in life. In fact the lesson stays with me to this day and grows deeper in meaning with each passing life experience. The story of Bob and me is a real-life account of how one man and his single-minded approach toward personal excellence changed not only my life, but that of my students as well.

I spent a good portion of my high school academic career (if you could call it that) in a highly indistinguishable manner. My portfolio was filled with largely inadequate works with the academic admonishments to back them up. While my peers and friends were vying for their places among the intellectual elite and the scholarship riches that come with them, I was mired in the basement, alone there with the stoners, dopers and other people your mother would warn you about (and my mother did). Unlike my counterparts, I was there not because of any significant deficiencies or self-destructive tendencies, but rather because I was lazy.

In my younger years, I was a model student – someone you could point to as a sign of future promise and expectations. I did my homework, participated in class and caused little to no trouble other than the occasional reprimand for an overactive mind and a mouth to match. At one point, I was even considered "gifted;" whatever that means. In the third grade I was tested and put in a self-contained classroom with the best and the brightest students in the school. I relished these experiences with my teacher and peers but felt largely inadcquate when compared to them. Sure, I was no dunce, but I never felt as if I belonged with those future type-A overachievers. I would soon prove this theory to be true.

I am not sure why or when exactly I stopped doing well in school. I have tried and I really can't remember, but somehow the straight A's of elementary school veered rather suddenly and inexplicably toward the latter part of the academic alphabet when I got to junior high. What used to be report cards to hail became report cards to hide. I knew I was capable of more, but just seemed to lack the desire to produce anything other than mediocre work. My parents did the usual threatening and grounding. They even utilized the familiar parental mantra of "how-are-you-going-to-get-into-a-good-college-with-these-grades?" This had little effect on my academic disposition. I was stuck in the middle of the bell curve on a good day and was sometimes seen sliding down the backside on other occasions. I was happy there. I saw no need to pursue greater heights.

"I knew I was capable of more..."

Believe it or not, my parents were right. My junior high grades were lacking to get into the high school of my choice (more my family's choice than mine), a highly prestigious religious academy nearby. Instead of choosing the local public high school, I chose another less-restrictive local private school as my backup, with the hope of returning to the promised land of private education for my sophomore through senior years. Continuing my pattern of laziness, I did little more than survive my freshman year at my new school. I even managed to fail Music Appreciation, which was taught by a psychotic elephant of a man who wore berets to school, which did little to dispel the high school myth (or not) of "band geek." During rehearsal he shouted out orders to the marching band like a tyrant and did little more the rest of the day other than read *Stereo Review Magazine* during class. If that was not pathetic enough, we were even required to complete quarterly reports after reading this scholarly periodical...THIS WAS HIGH SCHOOL MUSIC? My frustration was magnified when I learned that I was the only person in the class to fail. This was quite an accomplishment, given that the academic rigors were akin to that of a preschool.

My general unhappiness at the end of my freshman year led me to leave that situation, but my grades made it virtually impossible for me to go anywhere else other than my local public high school. This was all right by me, because it returned me to my stable of friends and to a place that had a more formidable music program, which was something of which I was growing increasingly fond. This would turn out to be a decision that would serve me well.

CAR GAME

Do you threaten your fellow students to get them to behave or practice?

How much negative reinforcement do you use versus positive?

Are you proactive or reactive in your pursuit of excellence?

I continued on through high school. My sophomore and junior years proved to be largely uneventful, with the exception of my newfound passion for music and my inability to rise to a higher standard in the classroom. I was certainly more than capable, but lacked the desire and discipline to utilize my skills for anything that did not meet my limited criteria of importance. This all changed the day I met Bob Larabell.

Mr. Larabell was a short and stout man whose gravelly voice only added to his charm and mystique. His perennial crew cut and dark-rimmed glasses gave him a more ominous appearance than his teddy bear physique would imply.

He had been teaching at this school for over twenty years and had developed a reputation as an instructor with unorthodox methods and extremely high standards. His grandfatherly tone and diminutive stature always reminded me of what Ernie from *Sesame Street* would look like if he were to grow old. Actually, Yoda from *Star Wars* would probably be a more accurate physical and intellectual representation of who and what he was. The subject he taught was A.P. College Composition, a one-semester course in academic suicide which would challenge even the most accomplished student, let alone a self-professed slacker like me. I got into the course through a scheduling glitch but decided to stay as the class contained most of my friends from band (where all of the smart kids were, in my opinion). This proved to be a pivotal decision that I would not regret.

From the first day, Mr. Larabell made his expectations quite clear. Every Monday, Wednesday and Friday, we would write a five-paragraph essay in one of various literary styles and re-work them on Tuesday and Thursday. This meant that he would grade twenty-two papers every single night of the week, and those were just from my class. He made it very clear that if we were to require so much of his time, he expected this time to be well-spent in the proliferation of our literary skills. Eventually, our continued writings would evolve into a thesis for a twenty-five page, typewritten, college-level thesis with five hundred annotated note cards and a one-hour oral defense in front of our peers. This was all to be done before the end of the first semester.

Normally, I am not one to brag, but I was impressive in this class, though not in the way you would think. Somehow, despite my track record of inconsistency, I was able to achieve a stature of regularity heretofore unmatched as I assembled forty-seven consecutive F's. Yes, that's right…forty-seven consecutive *failing* grades, and I have the papers to prove it. Sometimes it was my content, sometimes it was my grammar, but mostly it was a combination of all the above.

Regardless of the reason, I was mired in a level of ineptitude that frustrated even me beyond description. The pattern was simple: every other day, I would turn in a four-page essay, and Mr. Larabell would return it with so much red ink it looked like a Salvador Dali painting. Yes sir, forty-seven consecutive F's.

PICTURE MOMENT

Have you ever failed at something so spectacularly that you even surprised yourself? Have you ever failed at something and still enjoyed doing it? Have you ever been so consistent in your failure that you questioned what you were doing? How did you respond? Did you quit? Did you press on?

You can imagine how frustrated my parents were to discover their once-heralded, gifted child might in fact be a talentless idiot-in-waiting. My mother scheduled a meeting with Mr. Larabell and with me present, asked three straightforward questions to my teacher: "Why is he failing?", "Is he capable of the work?" and "Can he salvage the semester?"; to which Mr. Larabell retorted respectively, "Because he is lazy," "Absolutely," and "Yes, if he gets off of his butt and goes to work."

The message was clear. My mother turned to me and asked me what I wished to do. I responded that I wanted to stay in the class and tough it out. I knew it was the right thing to do and that the time for slacking off was over. The meeting ended and the gauntlet had been thrown down: I had to salvage my grade in the remaining three weeks of the semester or repeat the class next term.

Standing toe-to-toe with failure, I knew I had to make a choice, so I went to work. After all, I had fifteen weeks of sub-standard work to revisit, five hundred annotated note cards to complete and a twenty-page thesis paper to write. Sleep would not be an option. I worked nights, early mornings, weekends, and lunchtime. I even skipped school to spend all day in the library researching my chosen topic. If I was not in class or at my after-school job, I was writing – writing in the lunchroom, writing in my bedroom, writing in the park; and yes, writing in the bathroom (as gross as it sounds, every moment counted).

I managed to turn the F's into a D for the rough draft, a C for the final draft and even got a B on the oral presentation. With the completion of the paper and my success with the presentation I received a D and was not required to repeat the class. In his final written statement to me Bob Larabell wrote:

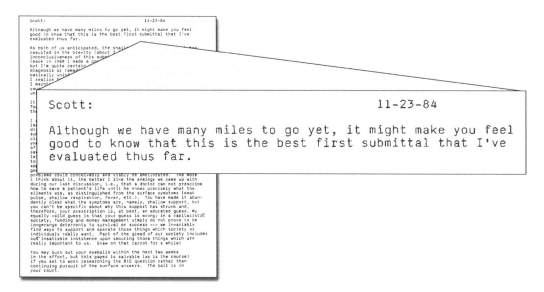

Scott: 11-23-84

Although we have many miles to go yet, it might make you feel good to know that this is the best first submittal that I've evaluated thus far.

I treasured that D, as it was something I truly had worked for and earned. I didn't care that it was not a higher grade, since I felt as if I had met the challenge head-on and stood toe-to-toe with a genuine obstacle and won – that is, if you count survival and a low C as a grade equal to "winning."

I would eventually graduate from high school and choose teaching music as a career, all the while knowing that I had derived a great deal of inspiration and personal pride from my daily battles with Mr. Larabell. I hoped to challenge my students just as he had challenged me, with dignity, respect and an unflinching standard of excellence.

My only regret was that I never told him how much he had meant to me and what a difference he had made in my life. Sure, I didn't come to the realization of his significance until after the cocoon of high school, but I always knew where to find him. Yet somehow, I never did.

 ### Fast forward fifteen years - August 2000

After a brief stint as an Assistant Principal, which is like a brief stint in prison (THERE IS NO SUCH THING), I returned to the classroom and was once again enjoying myself. I had found my niche as a motivator of youth and teacher of leadership skills. I loved teaching, not just because of the music, but because I loved challenging my students just as Bob Larabell had challenged me. As time passed and kids moved in and out of my classroom doors, the kind words and compliments from students were always accompanied by the sting of knowing that I had not done the same for my teacher. Even fifteen years after the fact, I still thought of him fondly and often, but sorely regretted not expressing my own gratitude.

Soon after this point I had the opportunity to move to a brand-new school and open a new music facility, an experience I still treasure to this day. Upon my arrival, I also soon became acquainted with the growing pains of a new facility, which included a few acoustical anomalies in my band room that would need to be addressed. I contacted the school's designing architect and was told that he would send someone to help on that coming Friday at 1:00.

On Friday, at one o'clock exactly, the door to my band room flew open. The raw sunshine that poured in and mixed with the fluorescent light was blocked only by a short, stocky shadow. As the door began to close the shadow turned into a person, and a recognizable face began to appear.

I stood there in disbelief as a figure from my past stood in front of me, reincarnated as an acoustical engineer. It was Bob Larabell, my high school English teacher. I came to find that prior to teaching he had been an Acoustical Engineer of quite some prominence, sold his house, and bought a condo so he could afford to start his life all over again as a teacher. After retiring from twenty-five years of teaching, he reestablished his business and returned to his once-forgotten profession. As we stood and discussed the acoustic situation, I tried to summon the courage to complete the task I had left unfinished a decade and a half ago. Knowing what I know about the importance of saying thank you did not make it easier to get the words out of my mouth. Somehow, he still had a stranglehold on me. My respect for him was so profound that even after all of these years I found it difficult to see him as a peer.

Our professional discussion came to a close and as he headed for the exit, the thought of letting another chance to thank him escape my grasp was enough to get me to blurt out, "MR. LARABELL!" He turned, and responded, "Yes?" I said, "Before you leave, I just need to tell you what an impact you made on my life. You probably do not remember me but I have been waiting over a decade to tell you this. Your willingness to stand up and hold me accountable for my actions made me understand not only what I could be, but also what kind of difference a teacher could make. You are one of the reasons I am a teacher today. I just wanted to say thank you."

He smiled in his grandfatherly way, said his "thanks", and continued his prolonged walk to the exit doors. As he reached the threshold of the door and once again allowed sunlight to enter the room, I stopped him once again. "Mr. Larabell…do you remember me?" He chuckled slightly and said, "Did you ever find a viable solution for the funding of the public arts [my thesis topic]?" Shocked and pleased with the ease at which he remembered my mediocre contribution to his class I answered with a smile, "NO." He responded, "I didn't think so," and walked out the door one last time.

As the sun-drenched door closed, and once again sunlight gave way to the fluorescent bulbs, a sudden peace came over me, as I was able to bring my long-held desire to thank him to a close.

I find it somewhat ironic that once again, even after fifteen years, he held me to a higher standard than I had held myself. He got me to do something I had been unable to do for so long: say thank you. Back then, he made me a better person and it continues even to this day.

 ## *The story continues…*

Recently I was asked to make a major presentation to some colleagues in the field of education at The Midwest Clinic. This was one of those "once-in-a-lifetime" experiences that could provide either a launching pad for success or serve as a crash site for failure. The pressure was on, and believe me when I say that I felt every ounce of it. In a last-minute panic attack, the day before the seminar I called a friend of mine from Tennessee, Terry Jolley, and begged him to help me get in the witness relocation program or to drug me with horse tranquilizers until it was all over, whichever would help the most. As he worked to calm me down, he suggested that I talk about Mr. Larabell as a part of the seminar. This struck me as odd, as I had mentioned this story to Terry in passing several years ago and was amazed that he even remembered it. I asked him why, to which he responded, "Because he reminds us of what we should be and can be and what we are." I was struck by the simple profoundness of what he said and went to work on changing the presentation to include the story of Bob and me.

> ## TRAVEL TIP
> It is much easier to thank someone while you are in the moment, rather than have to find them long after your paths have crossed.

As a way of keeping the story current, that next day, on my way to the airport, I tracked Bob down. Even though it had been five years since our acoustic encounter it was simple enough – one call to Information provided me with his current phone number and within minutes I was once again thanking him for the great influence he had on me. His dry wit and gravelly voice had not changed one bit, and as we spoke, I could visualize myself sitting in his classroom just as I had done some fifteen years earlier. It was an oddly comforting feeling. As a part of the conversation, he shared with me that moments earlier he had heard from another classmate of mine, Doug Atchison, who had written a screenplay based on the character of Bob Larabell and the teaching values he represented. It was a soon-to-be-released movie titled *Akeelah and the Bee*, with Lawrence Fishburne playing Bob Larabee, the character name for Bob Larabell. CAN YOU BELIEVE IT? I was shocked by the fact that someone would make a movie about my high school English teacher. I was also a little sad that someone was able to repay him for what he had done in a manner that I never could. Happy for him, but sad for me.

I joked with him about having Laurence Fishburne, a large African-American man playing Bob, a short white man, and proclaimed that if that was Hollywood's standard of realism, Brad Pitt should play me! After agreeing that Yoda was a more appropriate personality to play his role, we laughed and said good-bye. Obviously, I was not the only person upon whom this man had had his effect. Bravo, Bob!

Bob did not seek for me to be his best student. Bob just sought to find within me the best person that I could be. He was not concerned with how I stacked up against other students; he was just concerned as to how I stacked up against my potential.

I was lucky to have had the opportunity to encounter someone who believed in and demanded personal excellence, as it has transcended my high school experience and helped me throughout my life.

As if the story could get any more unbelievable, there is more, but that will have to wait until the next book.

 POSTCARD

Who are the teachers that have impacted your life?

Were they a classroom teacher, a coach, counselor, administrator?

What qualities did your teacher have that made an impact on you?

How did you change after having interacted with him/her?

When did you last talk?

Does this person know how you feel about him/her?

GIVE SOMETHING BACK

The best way to start a new journey is to revisit old ones and thank those who had a hand in making this leadership journey possible. Someone printed your ticket. Someone handled your luggage. Some kind stranger gave you directions when you were lost. **Even when alone, no one travels in solitude.**

I had the rare chance to go back and say a long awaited thank you to someone who meant a great deal to me. As a teacher, I have also been on the receiving end of these conversations and let me tell you, they are something you never forget. You need to seize this opportunity to give back to those who have given so much to you as you never know if you will ever get this chance again. I would like you to start the book on leadership with an act of gratitude to those who have embodied leadership to you. Sit down and write to the teacher(s) who have made an impact on your life, letting them know how much you appreciate them. Email and phone calls are expeditious and can serve in a pinch, but nothing says thank you quite like a handwritten letter. You have no idea what a difference it will make.

✸ TRAVELOGUE

CHAPTER ONE
Planning Your Trip

"Remember what Bilbo used to say: It's a dangerous business, Frodo, going out your door. You step onto the road, and if you don't keep your feet, there's no knowing where you might be swept off to."

J. R. R. Tolkien
English writer and author of the richly inventive epic fantasy *The Lord of the Rings*

Where are we, where do we want to go?

Creating a successful trip hinges on your ability to assess, prepare and plan, not only in regard to where you want to go but where you currently are. Think about it, a trip to Alaska looks a lot different to those of you living in Seattle than it does to those of you living in Florida. A trip to see the majestic Rocky Mountains looks a lot different to those who live in the plains of Nebraska

PICTURE MOMENT

Make a list of 25 things you love about your group. Tape the list to your locker or in a place where you can see it every single day. This will help to remind you to appreciate what you already have.

than it does to those who already live in Denver, Colorado. Not only is the planning and preparation of the trip affected, but so is your desire to make the trip at all. Are you as excited to see the beach when you live in California? Is the Grand Canyon as majestic to you when you live in the Grand Canyon State? Is the awesome spectacle of Niagara Falls as impacting when you see it every week? Things we experience in our everyday lives often lose their luster in becoming a part of the fabric of who we are. That does not mean that the Grand Canyon, Rocky Mountains or the sandy beaches are any less impressive or majestic, just that our day-to-day exposure to them has changed our perspective. That said, as we

PICTURE MOMENT

Remember, the place you call home is the same place someone calls vacation!

examine your journey, be sure to take a moment and appreciate what you currently have that you might be taking for granted. Remember, the place you call home is the same place someone calls vacation!

To that same end, the things that others may find special about your group, you may consider mundane. The things that others covet may be things that bother you. While other groups may wish to emulate the discipline and focus of your group, you would like your teacher to dial it down a little. Other groups may stand in awe of the 200 members in your organization and you wish your group were smaller, so that you could learn everybody's name. The old adage of "the grass is always greener on the other side of the fence," holds true in music groups as well. Before we begin charting a course and setting some goals, it is important to take stock of who you are, what you value and how you view success.

POSTCARD

What are the five things that other groups envy about your group?

What are five things that you envy about other groups?

You can't really set goals until you know how you define success, just as you cannot choose a path or vehicle until a destination is at hand. After all, a ship is not going to do you much good if you are trying to get from North Dakota to New Mexico, just as a car will fail you quickly when traveling from Boston to Frankfurt. A rickshaw will be of little value to you…well, JUST ABOUT ANYWHERE. I am sure that you get the point. Before we can move forward with choosing our destination and begin plotting our pathway, we must first determine where we are. Remember, it is much easier to see flaws in the places where you spend the most time, so try to be fair and see it from a "vacationer's" perspective before choosing your final answer.

The following pages contain a series of evaluation materials to help you determine where your leadership team and your group are at this point. Having a solid understanding of your starting point will not only help you clarify where you want to go (based on what you have already seen) but will also allow you to return back to the same point in the future and measure growth. These assessments can be taken throughout the year to determine where progress has been achieved and what course corrections may need to be made. It is important to be honest when filling this out and willing to see both the strengths and weaknesses of your group in an honest way. When you are done, compare your answers with everyone else in your group. If you are looking for a statistical norm, you can even average everyone's score.

Our leadership team is: (circle a number **and** a set of words)

on course		headed in the right direction			headed in the wrong direction				off course
1	2	3	4	5	6	7	8	9	10

Our student leaders are/were:

great tour guides		didn't get us lost			knew little about the area				got us lost
1	2	3	4	5	6	7	8	9	10

Our goals as a group are/were:

very clear		somewhat clear			not very clear			completely unclear	
1	2	3	4	5	6	7	8	9	10

Our leadership hierarchy was/is:

captain was on board		captain was a little lost			captain circled the airport			what captain?	
1	2	3	4	5	6	7	8	9	10

As the year progressed our team:

saw all the sights		saw the big stuff			could have seen more			never left the hotel	
1	2	3	4	5	6	7	8	9	10

Our current strengths as a program are:

(List a minimum of five. Be sure to include behaviors and values.)

Our current weaknesses as a program are:
(List a minimum of five. Be sure to include behaviors and values.)

In the past the people on the leadership team have been people who displayed: (circle all that apply)

dedication	compassion	caring	commitment	initiative	character
vision	risk-taking	ownership	cynicism	sarcasm	anger
patience	laziness	power hungry	shy	goal oriented	funny
productive	work ethic	honesty	lack of civility		

other:

This program is known for: (circle all that apply)

performance	character	innovation	excellence	mediocrity	caring
charity	personality	school spirit	friendliness	music	humor
manners	respect	pride	integrity	competitiveness	

other:

Our group needs to have more: (circle all that apply)

performance	character	innovation	excellence	focus	caring
charity	personality	school spirit	friendliness	music	competitiveness
manners	respect	pride	integrity	humor	integrity

other:

In the space provided, answer the following questions. Whenever possible, please try and make all answers as *specific* and *measurable* as possible. For instance, where it asks for your greatest hope, instead of writing, "Everyone be more dedicated," write "Our perfect attendance award increases by 10%," or "We increase our small group meetings to every week instead of every other week." The more measurable and specific your destination, the more likely you are to know it when you see it.

Time invested in travel:
How often do you meet? What can you personally commit?

Things that cannot be changed:
Facilities, personnel, location, hours in the day, resources (financial and otherwise), your budget, learning materials, faculty, and hired professionals.

Things out of our control:
Weather, student population, student demographics, field space, bell schedules, bus schedules, etc...

Equipment limitations:
What do you own, what do you have available to you? What is broken and in need of repair? What do you lack?

People involved in the trip:
Are there too many or too few? Are your job descriptions and responsibilities balanced and equal?

Strength of personnel involved:
List things that are strengths of the group as well as those that are not. Do people's job descriptions match their strengths and limit their weaknesses?

Past successes and failed endeavors of the program:
What are the historical strengths and weaknesses? What are things your group has traditionally prided themselves on, and what has your group failed at?

My greatest hope for this year's trip:

My greatest fear for this year's trip:

No matter what, we need to accomplish the following three things:

If things are going well, I would also like to see us address these things:

I would classify this journey as successful if:

I would classify this journey as a failure if:

Other thoughts I would like to discuss:

These assessments and the subsequent discussion of them should give you a good idea about your starting point both as a program and as its leadership team. As you process through all of the answers, don't get bogged down in specifics, or your agenda and ideas for improvement; that will occur later in the book. For right now, we are only worried about coming to consensus on where you are currently and where you would like to be when the process is done. **Simply stated, we are looking for a point of origination and a destination. When these two things have been discussed fully, you will be well on your way toward being an effective leadership team.** Remember, when choosing a destination there are no right or wrong locations. Keep in mind, however, that your dream destination of the North Pole may seem like a nightmare to someone wanting to absorb the sun on the beaches of Tahiti. As exotic as these locales may be, they would not suit the needs of a veteran spelunker looking to get some quality time inside a cave. Each group has its own individual identity and dreams. The destination can be whatever you want, just make sure everyone knows where you are headed and is willing to go there. Why is this important? Keep this in mind…

Next time you get on a plane, listen as the flight attendant makes the final call before closing the door. They always repeat the flight number and the destination. This always strikes me as funny. You would think the printed-out ticket, luggage check, gate check, and flashing sign at the boarding counter would serve to fend off any disengaged or irresponsible people seeking other destinations, but the smart flight attendant makes sure, just in case, because even though the likelihood of someone being on the wrong plane is small, the cost of the mistake is just too **BIG**! With that in mind…

LETS DO ONE FINAL CALL TO EVERYONE ABOARD AND MAKE SURE THEY ARE ALL ON THE RIGHT FLIGHT!

IF SOMEONE IS NOT ON THE RIGHT FLIGHT
(doesn't agree on where the group is headed)

GO BACK TO THE PLACE WHERE THAT PERSON GOT LOST

(in this book)

RETRACE YOUR STEPS

DO NOT MOVE FORWARD UNTIL EVERYONE IS ON BOARD!

At the risk of being painfully redundant, review the following five questions with everyone in the room before moving on with the next portion of the assessment.

TRAVEL ADVISORY

1. *WHERE ARE YOU?*
   What kind of shape is your group in?

2. *WHERE DO YOU WANT TO BE?*
   What kind of group do you want to have?

3. *DO YOU HAVE RESOURCES TO HELP?*
   Financial, intellectual, materials, personnel?

4. *HOW MUCH TIME DO WE HAVE?*
   A week, a month, a year, four years?

5. *IS EVERYBODY ON BOARD?*
   Parents, administrators, staff and students?

Choose three words from the list below that represent the terms you would use to describe a successful year. Put them in order of importance by ranking them individually and as a group. Tally the group vote and create a master list in order of importance to the group. Discuss the list with everyone before assigning numerical values and make sure everyone understands what they mean. Feel free to add other words. This activity should be done in groups of three or more.

awards   winning   accolades   charity   quality

individual growth   group growth   status   enrollment

trips/activities   challenges   fun   community service

school spirit   group bonding   marching   experience

concert   jazzguard   personal time   community service

group pride   inclusion   challenging materials

Additional words:

After you have tallied all of the votes for the small and the large groups, see if there are 2-3 items that stand out above the rest as being important to the members of your group/leadership team. These will serve as key descriptors as you begin to mold your definition of success. These will be your target goals or final destination. Don't worry if they seem vague; we can attach measurements to almost anything these days, so why not your final destination?

Now that we know what we view as success, how do we measure it?

When determining your destination or progress toward that end, there are a multitude of ways to do it. For instance, team athletics have wins and losses. Individual sports have personal bests, records and awards/accolades. Academically, we have scholarships, grade point averages, standardized test scores, and class rank to name a few. Even clubs can have tangible assessment using participation numbers, service projects and the like to determine their status in the developmental process, but music is a combination of all three: academics, athletics and activities. How do we build a rubric for success that represents all of these items? Does the rubric accurately reflect the daily activities of your group? To further complicate the process, there are varied areas of curricula and include jazz, concert, marching, and symphonic bands and percussion ensembles, which all need to be represented in the process. Notice that I did not say EQUALLY represented in the process. Their importance and hierarchy within your organization is a decision that you need to make based on your values, student needs and resources of your school community. You have to decide what is right for your program, given the circumstances of that year.

CAR GAME

You can use the qualifying words and/or mission statement to measure your success in a very concrete way. Listed below are some examples:

Awards - (self explanatory)

Accolades - Post emails and letters of congratulations. Count how many you receive. Make a goal to receive more.

Charity - How much money did you raise for needy groups this year? Grow the amount each year.

Personal Growth - Playing tests, honor group attendance, surveys, scholarships, GPA's, band grades.

Group Growth - Ratings and scores in all areas, recordings, comments from community.

Enrollment - Number of students, percentage of school, class counts, balance of seniors, juniors, etc...

Fun - Number of parties, birthday celebrations, holiday contests. (I always won the pumpkin-carving contest)

School Spirit - Win class competitions, pep assembly participation, tee shirts, posters, etc.

You get the idea. For every descriptor there is a way of measuring your progress. This can be done once a month, once a quarter, once a semester or once a year. You can involve just the leaders or the entire group. This is an excellent way for you to demonstrate growth to the group without using the all-too-common festival scores. Remember, you are the leaders of your group – chart a course, set sail, work hard and reflect on the journey every once in awhile.

CREATE A MISSION STATEMENT

Mission statements have become a staple of successful programs, businesses and multi-national companies. Their ability to succinctly articulate, inspire, motivate and communicate in a clear and concise manner the purpose of an organization has proven invaluable in the development of group identity and cohesion. Take the three words with the most votes from the list of words you choose to represent your program on the previous page and create a succinct and memorable mission statement. This statement should clearly reflect the values you will use to measure success. It is okay (in fact, encouraged) that your mission or parts of it change as your group changes.

Take the key words that received the most votes during the previous activity and place them in order of the votes they received. Use between three and six words and see if they make a sentence or act as a catalyst for a thought or theme. In an ideal world, the words should communicate a thought (or thoughts) with little alteration. However, you may need to make some slight adjustments to have the "message" of the mission statement speak in a clear and concise manner.

This can help to keep everyone on course and working together toward a clearly-stated common goal, especially during the difficult times. *If people can clearly see and identify an end result they can support, they will work harder, stay longer and endure more hardship.* This is why it is important to find commonly held beliefs and choose a unified destination. This activity may seem esoteric, when in fact it may be one of the most important activities in this text.

PICTURE MOMENT

When I did this activity with the Carmel High School Band in Indiana, this was their mission statement (the capitalized words were chosen by the students and placed in order of number of votes they received), I just added the word "for" in two places:

LOVE for BAND FAMILY, PASSION for EXCELLENCE

Beyond being a powerful statement about what they believe and its order of importance, specific and measurable behaviors can be attached to all of those words.

TRAVEL TIP

Once you have created your new mission statement, put it everywhere – posters, class handbook, programs, tee-shirts, etc... The more you invest in it, the more dividends it will return. This should provide a very clear, fairly concrete and measurable way for you to determine how you measure success and what you value in your group.

The joy of walking off the plane in the Hawaiian islands to a line of well-tanned and well-toned people who are ready to welcome you with a gentle kiss and a necklace of flowers may be somewhat tempered when you remember that you forgot to pack underwear. While garments alone do not make or break a vacation, they can definitely enhance or detract from it. Assess, plan and prepare for success...and remember, Wal-Mart has underwear real cheap in an emergency.

Am I the right Travelguide?

Now that we know where you are as a group and where you are headed, we have to decide if you are the right person to lead this journey. Think about it, Jacque Costeau (famous oceanographer) would make a horrible mountain guide and Sir Edmund Hillary (first person to climb Mount Everest) would be of little value to you on a scuba expedition. They are both leaders in their own right, but would not be as effective when placed in the wrong environment. In this way, I believe that leadership and being a travel guide have a lot in common. It is as much about being the right fit as it is about being a good leader.

With that said, are you the right travel guide (leader) for your group?

TRAVEL TIP

My dreams involve not only a location change but a physical change as well. I often picture myself as a bronzed, muscle-bound monster, rather than the pasty white Hobbit that I am.

When you dream about your vacation, are you prettier, thinner, happier, stronger, more outgoing, more adventurous?

Oftentimes while on a trip we pretend to be different than we are at home. We behave differently because of our vacation mindset. We might be freer, more relaxed or less inhibited than we might be at home.

Treat your leadership trip in a similar manner by trying to be a better person on the trip than you may be at home.

I think that sometimes the best part of a trip is not going on the trip but choosing the trip. You get to dream with an open mind about all of the possibilities of your adventure without dealing with the reality of lost luggage and sea-sickness. You also get to spend *months* planning your trip while the actual trip only lasts for *days*. I am one of those people who loves to plan almost as much as I love to do! I love looking through all of the brochures and Web sites showing my dream vacation, while I imagine myself swimming with sharks or scaling an eleven-thousand-foot mountain. Yes sir, I can practically see myself in those brochures; all muscle-bound and surrounded by beautiful….well, you get the point.

Each year brings about new and exciting opportunities for personal growth and group achievement within any organization. New members, new challenges, new objectives and new leadership provide a healthy sense of optimism among students and teachers alike. As the end of summer appears and the onset of school nears, there is a palpable sense of passion and excitement in the air. The same sense of energy can be felt in the spring as new leaders are chosen and a bridge is built to the next school year. Great expectations and a sense of single-minded purpose fill each meeting and group gathering. This is the time for dreamers and visionaries to create something truly special.

Dreaming is my favorite time in the leadership development process. I do not think we dream enough in our lives. I believe that we worry more about minutiae than the bigger picture. While the mundane, day-to-day tasks are crucial to the success of a group, they do not stir our souls, move our hearts or capture our imaginations. It was two dreamers who created Google. It was a guy in his garage named Steve Jobs who ultimately created the iPod. MySpace and YouTube were once fleeting thoughts conceived in the middle of the night by people just like you and me. The only difference is that they brought their dreams to the light of day.

In a different vein, it was Martin Luther King's stirring of our souls that put us on the path to equality for all and John Fitzgerald Kennedy who captured our imaginations and subsequently put a man on the moon. The ability to dream, to create a vision for the future, is an important and often overlooked element of the leadership process. It is a skill to be sure. Some may find it easier to do than others, but we all at least have the ability to dream. Dreaming is certainly not doing, but that does not invalidate the need for it. Yes, dreaming is a skill. And yes, it comes easier to some more than others, but everyone can do it. So, let's take a moment and do just that.

 POSTCARD

Who is your favorite dreamer?

What did they create?

Who created something you wish you had created?

Who inspires you to think beyond the realm of the obvious and predictable?

What would you like to create?

Begin by clearing your mind of "what is" to help you prepare for "what can be." Oftentimes the day-to-day realities of a situation overwhelm and overshadow the opportunities and solutions that are within our grasp. The easiest way for me to do this is to imagine that I could be responsible for the recreation of a particular situation or scenario. I then ask myself, "If I were to recreate this from scratch, trying to achieve the best results possible, how would I do that?" For instance, if I were to dream of the perfect rehearsal, would it be indoors or outdoors? How long would it be? How would it be structured? Who would be there? What would the structure be like? You get the idea. After I have dreamed the perfect rehearsal, I examine what my current rehearsals look like and attempt to bridge the gap between the two. This process allows me to strip away any ties that bind in search of a more efficient and effective way of doing things. Are there obstacles to my

PICTURE MOMENT

Find your dream first; tackle its obstacles next.

THE TIES THAT BIND

Please use the space provided to answer the questions below as it relates to your specific group this year.

What are the ties that bind your group: rehearsal time, space, equipment, money, facilities, talent, etc.?

Take a moment and reflect on what the REAL ties are and which of these can be addressed and altered to better the group. Make a list of everything that comes to mind. After each binding item list three things you can do you either eliminate the issue or lessen its negative impact on your group.

NO IDEA IS TOO INSIGNIFICANT, so really think through your answers.

Do this first then discuss them as a group afterwards.

In the previous chapter, you wrote down some thoughts as to how you would view and assess whether or not last year was a success. If you did not discuss them as a group, now would be a good time. Be sure to listen to the answers of your peers, as it will provide a keen insight on what the culture of your group is and help you to understand what you can do to be a service to that mission.

As you will come to find, this workbook places a premium on the individual components of leadership and group dynamics. Your group may be an effective group, and you may be an effective leader, but that does not mean that you will be an effective leader for that group during this given time frame. Leadership roles are as much about building and maintaining relationships as they are about seeking out and accomplishing tasks. Predicting your level of success in that role is as dicey as predicting how successful a marriage might be. No matter what the evidence may suggest, you have about a 50/50 shot of being wrong. It is like predicting the sex of a baby or the flip of a coin – yes, there are predictors and indicators of success, but there are no guarantees. We all have seen seemingly perfect relationships go sour while those facing seemingly insurmountable odds flourish. The same can be said for the role of a leader. Given all of your preparation and indicators of success, it is quite possible you will not meet with the success you might expect. What is the difference between the two? What can bridge the gap between a successful relationship and a failed one? I would answer this: the same things that can bridge the gap between a successful leader and a failed one – communication, commitment, caring and sacrifice. Each one of these qualities unto themselves could fill an entire book if not a library, but for the purpose of this book, ask yourself the following questions:

TRAVEL ADVISORY

1. Communication:

Do I communicate with those I am leading? Is it more positive or negative? Is it more proactive or reactive? How can I improve?

2. Commitment:

How committed am I to this group? Is this my first priority at school? If not, where is it in my spectrum of priorities? Are those in my charge more committed than I am? Do I come early, stay late and volunteer for tasks when asked?

3. Caring:

Do I genuinely care for those I am leading? Is my level of caring based on their level of talent or contribution? Do I care about them outside of this group? Do they care for me more than I care for them?

4. Sacrifice:

If I am to add on these additional responsibilities, what am I willing to give up? Am I willing to sacrifice personal gain for the group gain? Am I willing to sacrifice my time and energy without acknowledgement or reward?

These are all important questions worthy of some serious and honest introspection. <u>Now might be a good time to put down the book and think about these questions.</u> There are no right answers, just honest ones. No one expects you to be a saint, so it is natural and understandable to fall short in one or more of the areas listed above. Just make sure you are aware of it and are making strides to improve. That is all we can ask of you as a person and as a leader.

 ## COMPARE AND CONTRAST

On one side of the line, make a list of your three greatest strengths and weaknesses as a leader. On the other make a list of responsibilities for the position you serve in. Compare and contrast the two to see if you are a good fit for your position. When you are done, show it to your teacher and ask for feedback.

On the previous page, were you honest and unbiased in your assessment? Are you prepared to bridge the gap between who you are and who you want to be? If so, let's move forward by asking two key questions:

1. What is the culture of your group?

2. Is my leadership style a good fit for the group?

PICTURE MOMENT

This would be a good time to stop reading and think. If your answer to these questions is flawed, so is the rest of your work in this book.

Are these simple questions? Yes. Sound overly simple? Maybe. Is getting the necessary information to answer these questions going to be easy? NO. As you know, each person has a unique genetic makeup that differentiates them from the billions of people who have come before and the billions who are to follow. Mathematical probability tells us there are no two identical people on this planet. Even in identical twins, created from the same genetic material and raised in the same household, there will be significant differences. The same can be said for each organization. **There are no two identical organizations on the planet, even if they are from the same city, the same school or have the same teacher/sponsor.** The personal makeup of the group, the students, creates a wholly individual organization that changes from year to year, even when all other factors remain unchanged.

A good friend of mine, David Duarté, resigned a teaching position he once coveted, after eight treacherous months in which he found little joy. After leaving what he thought was his "dream job," he vowed he would never teach again and actively pursued other non-teaching musical opportunities. In short, his teaching career was over. Three months later, a desperate situation at another school and a kind, caring heart led him to return, "just for a year to help out." Five years later, he is still there and has built a jazz program that has won several national contests and has been invited to play at the *Monterey Jazz Festival* and *The Midwest Clinic*. It turns out that teaching was what he wanted to do, but his previous school was a bad fit.

This is all a very roundabout way of saying that you are an individual with your own views on leadership and special skills. Your group has its own student leadership needs. The fact that someone chose you to lead your group means that he or she believed you to be a person who can be effective in a leadership role. The fact that you accepted the invitation means that you believe in the promise and possibility of the group. What remains to ask yourself is this: "Are my leadership skills and talents a good match for the group? Can I help make this a better organization than before? If so, how?"

This is what the remainder of this book and training process will focus around: the development of your leadership skills, the group's value systems, and how to marry the two for the good of everyone involved. This is very important, but we have gotten off subject a little – let's get back to dreaming and some activities to get you started!

DREAM COLLAGE

A dream collage serves as a visual reminder for the things you want to pursue. It allows you to keep your dreams in sight, both literally and figuratively. It is a fun way for you (and your students) to get your creative juices flowing and can serve as a great discussion starter or leadership activity with your leadership team or entire ensemble.   When I did this activity with my students, I broke them up into small teams and asked them to begin the activity by brainstorming what they thought the perfect ensemble looked like. After their collages were complete, we had each group present them to the entire group. After everyone had finished presenting, we had a discussion on which elements were common among all collages and which elements stood out. The collages were hung throughout the entire leadership weekend and they served as a reminder for what we were striving for. You can even hang the collages throughout your rehearsal space to serve as a visual cue for the entire ensemble. The students really had fun with this activity.

For this activity, you will need a collection of old magazines (travel magazines are fun), scissors, glue, and any other art supplies (construction paper, drawing tools) that they will need to make a collage. Keep in mind, the more obscure the magazine (Spandex Wearing Bass Fishers Quarterly) the more the kids had to stretch to find materials for the project and the more we laughed.

After giving the students the materials, ask them to use pictures from the magazines to make a collage of all the things they want in and for their group: Happiness, commitment, dedication, talent, equipment, trips, awards, etc...

Encourage the students to let their imaginations run wild. Tell them to include all the things, big and small, that they dream of having or being. Then explain that they'll use their collages to work out some of the goals on the following page.

HAVE FUN WITH THIS AND ENJOY THE EXPERIENCE.

DREAM TEST

Some people are better dreamers than others. Some people enjoy daydreaming and fantasizing more than others. Some people find it easier to think outside of the box and get creative than others. I am not talking about drool on the pillow, can't remember it in the morning type dreams, I am talking about the dreams you have when you are awake...well sort of. I am talking about the thoughts that dance around in your head during English class. I am talking about the thoughts that entertain your mind as you run laps in gym class. If you believe in dream analysis, you know that the dreams you have represent your unconscious mind. I am more interested in the dreams you have in your conscious mind...DAYDREAMS.

As you prepare to lead, you must daydream about it. There is some small space in your mind which thinks about the "what ifs" and the "can do's". These dreams help serve as fuel for the imagination and are something of a GPS (Global Positioning Satellite) for your mind. They keep you energized when times are tough and headed in the right direction when your head is foggy. However, when left unattended and ignored, they can leave you listless, going nowhere and without any energy. Daydreaming is good. Daydreaming can help, so let's take a moment and see what kind of daydreamer you are.

Are you a realistic leader? Are you a daydreamer who can't put dreams into action? Are you someone who is always thinking about the "what if" instead of the "what is?" Are you preparing for success or just dreaming about it? Now is the chance to find out. Give yourself a point for each question you answer yes to and then tally your score.

DREAM TEST

_____ 1. Do you have a different dream for every day of the week?

_____ 2. Do you judge your dreams by whether your friends will approve?

_____ 3. You spend more time talking about your dream to your friends than doing something to make it happen?

_____ 4. Are you are more likely to dream about being in a better group than do something about it?

_____ 5. Do your dreams usually revolve around being conductor of the Boston Symphony or something equally grandiose? Do you dream about the perfect performance but fail to submit to the necessary rigors to achieve it?

_____ 6. Are your dreams an escape from your leadership role rather than an inspiration for it?

_____ 7. Do you think that your dreams would come true if it weren't for the laziness of others? Do you blame others for your lack of success?

_____ 8. Do you find that the more you think about your dreams, the more frustrated you are with your current group?

_____ 9. Are quick to abandon one dream for another?

_____ 10. Do you refuse to adjust your dream even when it is not working with your current situation?

_____ 11. Do you have a thousand ideas on how to make other groups better but you don't use any of them with your own group?

_____ 12. Do you see yourself as the one in the spotlight rather than operating it?

DREAM TEST SCORING

0-4 points: You don't fly often. You prefer to be on the ground. You have a realistic approach to grounded dreams. You are thoughtful and reflective but balanced. You are making positive steps toward making your organization a better one.

5-8 points: You are a seasoned flier and know the best way to get from point A to point B. You are a dreamer at heart who sees the group he wants rather than what he has. Strike a balance between the two and watch the group flourish.

9-12 points: You are a frequent flyer. There is no avoiding it, you are a dreamaholic. You can dream; the question is, are you committed to really making your dreams happen? Remember, dreaming should enhance your group, not frustrate you. Focus on a few attainable dreams and move forward with just those.

ALONG THE WAY...

TRY IT ON BEFORE YOU BUY IT
Make sure your plane is headed where you want to go.

How do you know if your concert tux is going to fit? You try it on and wave your arms around as if you were conducting the Mahler V. As silly as you may look to others, it is what is required to ensure the proper fit and feel. The same should be done with your dream...you need to "try it on" and see how it fits and how it feels. Does the thought of it make you excited or make you tired? Does it make you lie awake at night in anticipation or in palpitations? Does the same dream reoccur on multiple nights? Before you can completely decide if you want to own your dream vacation, you should first make sure you can handle the weather.

ALONG THE WAY...

SHARE WITH CARE
Don't carry someone else's baggage.

Sharing your dreams is an act of faith. You should only share them when you are ready and only with those who will be supportive. There is a time and place to pass it around for the naysayers and realists for examination, but this is not the time. If you believe that you can hike Mt. McKinley or swim with sharks along the Great Barrier Reef, then at first, share it with those whom you know will be supportive and help point you in the right direction.

Dreams have a gestational period, much like a pregnancy. Within the entire ten-month process (the length of a school year including pre-school rehearsals) are three distinct trimesters. Like a pregnancy, when you first find out, you don't tell the world, just the people closest to you. After a period of time, safety concerns are alleviated and the appearance of the newborn becomes more concrete. At this time, your circle of communication widens. Finally, when the event is imminent and obvious to one and all do you share your joy with the world? There is a time and place to tell those around you what you are dreaming...just remember, discretion is the better part of valor.

ALONG THE WAY...

START LIVING YOUR DREAM A LITTLE AT A TIME
Each great vacation starts with saving a little bit each day to pay for it.

If your dream is to take your group to a national competition, start by going yourself and attending the director preview activities. After which, call some of the directors whose groups experienced success and ask them for their recommendations and tips. It would probably be best to speak with those whose groups are most like yours in philosophy and makeup. Don't visit with a director of an urban program with nine staff members and 350 students if you are from a small rural school where the principal also drives the school bus. It might be interesting but not applicable. Find someone who has a program like yours that has reached that level of success and ask them how they did it. It will be more fruitful and less frustrating.

You could make the leap from where you are to the national stage...but would you be less likely to be successful in the long run? That could prove to be hurtful not only to your dream but also, more importantly, to your students. Dreaming is not the most pragmatic of ways to spend your days, but planning for your dreams is the only way to ensure success. Are you preparing for success?

TRAVEL BROCHURES LIE

The very essence of capitalism is to provide a product or service, establish a cost, and hope that consumers will find value in it. In theory, the more innovative and value based your idea is, the greater your economic success. In pursuit of success, sometimes the truth gets stretched a little…OR A LOT! Brochures will go out of their way to show you sandy beaches but fail to mention the cannibals that live on the island. Web sites will highlight all of the amenities but neglect the fact that it is a six-hour camel ride from the airport to the hotel. The concept of highlighting the positives and ignoring the negatives (lying) applies to virtually every part of your life, including your group. Think about the time of year when teachers try to recruit new students for marching band. We say, "Join band…it will be FUN!" We don't mean to lie, but go out of our way emphasize the positive rather than the negative effects of your participation. We tell you about the many friends you will make but skip the part about the smelly uniforms. We tell you about the many trips you will take but conveniently fail to mention the yellow bus you will be taking them in. We mention the "pride" you will feel but not the part where your sweaty underwear starts to ride up on you during one of your marathon rehearsals. Is it lying or creative information disbursement? You be the judge. In the end though, we all share in the belief and hope that through your participation your life will be enhanced in some small way.

CAR GAME

Sit down and make a top ten list out loud of lies that are told to your group...like, the five-minute water break that is only one minute, or the famous, "Hey kids, let's do it ONE MORE TIME." Make the final list into a poster for the entire group. This will show everyone that you recognize some of the truth stretching that goes on and are able to laugh at it.

This book works in a similar manner as it deals mostly with the positive aspects of your leadership journey. It is my sincere hope that after your travels, you will find something of value that will enhance your life (or has already) and will make future trips even more enjoyable. It is possible though, that you will consider reading this travel guide a significant waste of time and of little value to your life. In the end, all I can do is point out my travel philosophies and be as honest as possible about why I think they will be of value to you in your travels. Will I forget something? Yes. Will I choose to emphasize some things over others? Yes. Should my beliefs be the same as yours? NO. Having said that, below are two lists:

What to Expect and What Not to Expect from this leadership journey:

What to Expect
You will make new friends.
You will lose some friends.
You will create life memories.
You will have diverse and challenging experiences.
You will grow and learn more than your peers who are not leaders.
You will be more successful in future endeavors.
You will learn more skills.
You will laugh more.
You will cry more.
You will sleep less.
You will work more.
You will see the best and worst in others.
You will see the best and worst in yourself.

What Not to Expect
You will not find a series of magical steps to make you a leader.
You will not find platitudes that will fit all persons and all journeys.
You will not find absolutes.
You will not find this book to be a simple exercise in reading.
You will not get something from this unless you give something to it.
You will not gain as much from this book if you complete it individually.
You will not find yourself agreeing with me on everything.

CAR GAME

Have you ever thought about writing/publishing something? How about a children's book for leaders? Create a group Web site or a brochure for your organization. Use ideas and layouts from travel Web sites. After all, they have spent a lot of money trying to lure you in, why not take advantage of that?

Do we tell you these things when you sign up to be a leader? Do we give you a fair and fully accurate picture of what to expect before you step in front of your peers? Most likely not. Oftentimes students choose leadership positions based on what they have witnessed from the outside of the previous leadership teams. Before joining, they rarely ask questions, rarely sit in on meetings to gain more information and almost never interview the sponsor to learn more about expectations. They just make an educated guess and take a giant leap of faith. This is like choosing a six-week vacation based on a thirty-minute infomercial. Remember that infomercials are often light on information and heavy on commercial.

TRAVEL ADVISORY

What did you really know about the position before you applied for it?

How does it compare with the actual job?

I hope that you will take some time to add to the leadership list and email it to me. I know you are far more creative than I am and you never know when it might appear in print. If you are not ready just yet, wait a little while and revisit this chapter. By then, you may have enough material to write your own book. Your own personal experiences will allow you to create a list as unique as you are. After rereading your list, are you still sure you want to make the trip?

Call it marketing, call it creative recruiting, call it lying, call it what you will. We all try and accentuate the positives and play down the negatives. There is no perfect vacation. There is no perfect destination. There are no perfect organizations. We do know that once someone has made the choice to make the trip by joining your group, it is one that they will never forget nor regret. Like leadership, traveling is nothing more than a series of opportunities and choices that allow us to create the experience of your choice.

BRAINSTORMING

Place large pieces of butcher paper on the walls of your room. At the top of each piece, write a question or a thought that you would like the students to respond to. You can do this with just your leadership team or your whole group. Have everyone write a response to the questions on a sheet of paper. You can make this a timed or un-timed activity, depending on the number of participants. The instructions and questions can change with the group.

This activity can be done with two people or two hundred people. All you need is people with ideas and butcher paper. The rest is up to you and your creativity. You can even do this activity multiple times a year and use the results as brainstorming to build a better group.

For more sincere answers and better accountability, have the students sign their statements. This activity will be a great idea generator and discussion starter but may also show people how differently the same trip can be viewed by others.

Listed below are just a few sample thoughts to get your creative juices flowing.

Favorite part of being in the group
Least favorite part of being in the group
Best day in the group
Worst day in the group
Favorite music to play
Tasks which need to be done to make us better
Better ways to run a sectional
Fundraising ideas
Spirit ideas
Motivational quotes
Promises to themselves

Etc...

During workshops, I often ask students if they know someone who loves their school. Obviously, hands fly into the air. I then ask them if they know someone who does not like their school. Believe it or not, usually, more hands rise than did for the previous question. I remind the students that school is nothing more than brick and mortar and their experience is what they choose to make of it. The same thing can be said for your ensemble.

PICTURE MOMENT

There are those in your group who will have a great experience this year and those who will not. In the end, the one who most controls the quality of the experience is YOU!

Use these lists (butcher paper with responses on it) to have an honest conversation about the state of the organization and how each individual can work to make the whole group better. You can spend some time studying all of the statements or have the students pick out some ones they would like to discuss. This can be a frank exchange among leaders, an open-ended discussion with the director, or all of the above. This will help dispel some of the myths, innuendo and yes, lies that we tell in our groups. In the end, it will lead to a happier, more productive group that has more fun...I guess we didn't lie after all!

PACKING LIST

List three things you learned about yourself in this chapter:

List three things you need to "pack" for your leadership journey:

List three things you learned about the journey that is ahead of you:

Write a little bit about what you value most about your group:

Write a little bit about what you value the least about your group:

 # TRAVELOGUE

CHAPTER TWO
Before You Travel:
The Basics

...I shall be telling this with a sigh

Somewhere ages and ages hence:

Two roads diverged in a wood, and I –

I took the one less traveled by,

And that has made all the difference.

Robert Frost

The Commercialization of Leadership

As a general rule, I don't like commercials. I know I am not alone in this, as all of the friends I have asked share my opinion. And yet, still they persist. The way I see it, these mini infomercials are of little value and serve no purpose in our lives other than the occasional belly laugh.

We Americans commercialize everything. Even commercials have commercials within them. Ever seen an ad for pizza where a soda is prominently displayed next to the pizza with the logo facing out? Ever been to a movie where the characters seem to go out of their way to use a certain computer or drive a certain brand of car? This is no accident. Some ad campaigns are covert and some are overt, but the end result is the same: someone is going to great lengths to get my attention.

PICTURE MOMENT

I find this quite interesting: To think that hundreds of companies line up to pay millions of dollars to have thirty seconds of MY time both insults and empowers me.

In the end, I figure if they are going to spend that much money on me, it would be rude for me to ignore them, and so I dutifully do my best to give them the attention they deserve. Seriously, when you think about it, the amount of money, time, and effort spent on me by my boss pales in comparison to what Wal-Mart and Proctor and Gamble spend, logically speaking. That means I should spend a little less time paying attention to my boss and a little more time paying attention to my television, right?

That said, I will still stand by my previous statement – I don't like commercials. Beyond their absurdity is their sheer volume. Thanks to Tivo, I recently timed an hour of television and found that only forty minutes was actual programming, while the remaining twenty minutes consisted of advertisements. That means one third of all television events are ads. What a waste! Thank goodness for Tivo.

There is one exception, however. I recently watched the Super Bowl, which is the epitome of "commercialtainment." It is the Emmys, Oscars and MTV Awards all wrapped into one. This is the one time of year I can actually enjoy commercials as I watch companies pull out all of the stops to get my attention. In fact, my understanding is that large quantities of the viewing public watch the Super Bowl just for the ads. There are even entire Web sites and online polls which serve no other purpose other than to gauge the world's reaction to these multi-million dollar "mini-movies." To be honest, this year I actually Tivoed the game so I wouldn't miss any of the commercials. I did not want to be the only one at school the next day left out of the loop and wondering what everyone else was talking about. As a music teacher, I have a hard enough time making friends without adding isolation to the equation.

Everything in the Super Bowl has a sponsor, including the two-minute warning. Yes, this past year, the two-minute warning was brought to you by GoDaddy.com – as if without them, we would have not had the two-minute warning. Frankly, the two-minute warning is boring. I wish GoDaddy had not sponsored it and spent their money sponsoring more shots of the marching band. Talk about value for your dollar. Think about it: GoDaddy presents – two minutes with the marching band. I would support that company!

 **POSTCARD**

What is your favorite commercial of all time?

What is the most memorable commercial of all time?

Are they one and the same?

What made you respond to them...humor, shock, music, star power, etc.?

What are the things that are effective in swaying your opinions or altering your belief systems?

Next time you are watching television, really watch the advertisements, not just for their content, but for the context in which they are shot. Who are they marketing to and how does that alter their approach? This would be a fun leadership group discussion.

Commercials are sometimes boring, sometimes poignant and oftentimes comical. The best commercials are the ones that have it all…drug commercials. I love pharmaceutical commercials. You know, the ones that spend twenty-eight seconds telling you how their product can transform your life for the better only to tell you in the final two seconds how it might also impair or even end it in print so small and shown so fast that it would take a mosquito on Red Bull to read it. These pharmaceutical commercials are GREAT.

It's not the sweeping views of beautiful people standing on cliffs that I enjoy; it's not the romantic music in the background. It isn't even the hope that through these medications we can improve the quality of life for someone who is suffering. It is the disclaimers at the end. Yes, the disclaimers – you know, the stuff the announcers read really fast and quiet at the very end hoping that you don't notice what is being said. They seem to be convinced that you are so excited about the possibility of ending the discomfort of acid reflux disease that you are not going to notice or care about the fact that it can cause sudden loss of appetite, dizziness, mild bowel discomfort and possible death – yes, in some extreme cases, DEATH. I have suffered from a bad case of acid indigestion. I even believed at one time that I had acid reflux disease, but I will take the temporary and mild inconvenience of this when compared to a visit from the Grim Reaper.

As I said, I enjoy the disclaimers. I am always amused at how nicely they can describe the side effects of certain medications and somehow note that it is only POSSIBLE that you may die. (As if you might not notice or care if the hair loss medicine you are talking might induce a visit from the Grim Reaper.) I doubt that adding the five-second "tag of death" is something they are doing out of the goodness of their own hearts. I know it is out of government regulation. I guess I should be calling and thanking my local Congressperson, not for their efforts to ensure my safety, but for providing me with some amusement as I watch Jerry Springer. I know that somewhere among the millions and millions of pages of legislative script there is something somewhere in small print that requires full disclosure among advertisers about the side effects of using their products. Somehow, cigarette and alcohol manufacturers seemed to have escaped this directive, but that is for another book. In general, I think these disclaimers are a good idea. They keep people informed and keep the manufacturers somewhat honest.

I wish more things in life required a disclaimer. I think all travel brochures and leadership guides should have them as well. I think this would help people avoid some of the poor decisions they make, myself included. I wish I knew about the six-hour car ride before I chose the resort in Jamaica my wife and I honeymooned at. I wish I knew that the airport in Denver was forty miles from civilization before I got stuck there for 36 hours. I REALLY wish someone would have posted a disclaimer keeping me from some of the people I dated. It would have saved me time, money and embarrassment, not to mention the anxiety of wondering if I would get stalked after a bad breakup. Disclaimers are important as they often shed some light on the TRUTH. Imagine what the disclaimer might be for parenthood…

WARNING!

> A child may result in two years of day-and-night diaper duty, sleep deprivation, anxiety, frustration, a sudden loss of language skills and ability to reason. Exposure to odd smells and textures are certain as a result of the child experiencing sudden fluid loss simultaneously from all possible body sources. Those who come into contact should immediately seek professional help from a qualified professional prior to incurring irreversibledamage to their emotional and physical well being.

That would be enough to make me think twice about reproducing. HECK…If I knew then what I know now, I might have considered enrolling in divinity school and heading off to a monastery for awhile before I became a father.

CREATE A DISCLAIMER

Wouldn't that be great if people came with a disclaimer? What would your disclaimer say about you? Write one for you and one for your friends and compare them.

Can you imagine what life would be like if we knew where decisions would lead?

- *Would Hitler have invaded Europe had he known the outcome?*
- *Would Kennedy have become President if he had known he would have to pay the ultimate price?*
- *Would we currently be involved in the Middle East?*
- *Would you have voted differently in the last election?*
- *Would you have chosen the job where you are currently employed?*
- *Would you wear your seat belt more often and drive more slowly?*
- *Do you think that if everyone had read a full disclaimer of owning a pet that we would have as many animal shelters as we do now?*
- *Do you think that the number of drunken driving incidents would be the same?*
- *Do believe for one minute that we would have as many people abusing drugs if they had clearly understood what the ramifications of their decisions were? I doubt it!*

I think the same things can be said for leadership. I think that young people are dazzled by the "commercialization" of leadership and are drawn by the title and perceived power. There is the appeal of the speech in front of their peers, the accepting of awards and the popularity associated with being at the forefront of an organization. I believe that prior to assuming a position of leadership we should make young people read a disclaimer.

If we were to require this, what would the disclaimer look like? What would it say? What would it warn you about? Perhaps it might look something like this:

WARNING!

Leadership may be accompanied by a sudden loss of friends, an overly acute sense of self worth, sensitivity to critical remarks, and a possible loss of perspective. Side effects may include sudden loss of sleep, irritable life syndrome, stress, discomfort, paranoia and general frustration.

If we marked this disclaimer on every leadership application, would we have the same amount of applicants? Would our journey be less crowded? Would the caliber and/or quantity of students seeking leadership positions be different? Would the caliber of adults who call themselves leaders be different?

Just as with pharmaceuticals, the benefits of leadership oftentimes outweigh the detriments, but in some cases and with some people, the risks of leadership are simply not worth the struggles. The choice has to be made by the individual, after a full disclosure of the benefits and the drawbacks of leadership. There is no one-size-fits-all solution to leadership.

There is no prescription for excellence that comes without side effects.

Are you prepared for them? Are they worth it to you?

COMMERCIALIZATION OF LEADERSHIP

1. List the possible damaging effects of leadership, both personal and organizational.

2. Which one scares you the most?

3. In a group, write your own disclaimer for leadership.

4. List the possible benefits of leadership as if it were to appear in a commercial. Be sure to act as if you really are selling it – ham it up! Lying would be unethical and inappropriate but stretching the truth will make it far more entertaining.

CREATE A COMMERCIAL

Using a small group of people, make and perform a one-minute commercial promoting leadership or your group in general and what it can offer the group that uses it. The commercial must contain a brief disclosure at the end containing the possible harmful "side effects" of being a leader. (Hint: pick someone who can memorize this part and read it really fast; this can produce hilarious results. The more outrageous the side effects, the better.) When you are done, pop some popcorn and perform the commercials. You can even have awards for the best commercials, complete with acceptance speeches.

WE LIED TO YOU:
We Really Don't Want Leaders, We Want Followers!

The number one complaint that I hear as I work with teachers and students from all across the country is the lack of leadership that young people display. Almost without exception, program directors and teachers feel that with better student leadership, the combined experience of the group and its leadership would be a better one for everyone involved. Your educational experience would be richer and the content would be deeper and more meaningful. So if we know what a powerful tool student leadership can be and we know that people would like to see more of it in their programs, then…

- *Why don't we teach it in classes?*
- *Why don't we invest more time in it?*
- *Why don't we seek out and reward leadership behaviors?*

 POSTCARD

What is your number #1 complaint about being a leader in your group?

What can you do to make it better?

Make a list right now of five things you and your leadership team can do to make a difference. See how your complaint matches up to others.

The answer to these questions is a window to a much larger issue – the issue of culture.

Everyday we ask you, the students, to conform to and follow *ALL* the rules: arrive on time, follow the dress code, don't run in the hallways, get a pass/permission slip before going anywhere, be quiet while the teacher is talking, sit up straight, practice, put your instrument up when we tell you, down when we say, play when we say, play how we say, always have your supplies, etc. In fact, most teachers (myself included) print out a multi-page manifesto of rules and regulations to distribute to students at the start of each year. This volume goes to great lengths to outline what students should NOT do, more so than what they *should* do. This is pretty amazing when you consider the fact that most music organizations' handbooks are greater in volume than the Constitution, Declaration of Independence and the Bill of Rights COMBINED! All of this is in addition to the student handbook that the school prints out and requires each student to sign and agree to. **Ironic that we seem to require more material to run our third-period class than was required to establish the most powerful nation on earth, isn't it?**

CAR GAME

Be honest! Which rule in your group do you "fudge," finesse or just ignore?

As a teacher, I got in trouble a lot for not taking attendance. Go around the room and share your "fudge" factor. There of course has to be guaranteed immunity from prosecution (your teacher)!

TRAVEL ADVISORY

Time for a revolution! As an exercise, revolt against the tyrannical handbook and reduce it to a one page document. Spend some time thinking about what is really important and include it. Of course this does not mean one continuous roll of paper with a seven point font. It means, get to the heart of the issues and say only what needs to be said in a clear and concise way. This will help you to define your core values, even if you choose not to use it. This will be an interesting exercise. You can do this as individuals, small groups or as a whole.

As I mentioned, music teachers are among the most egregious offenders of the tree-killing clan. We have made an art form of detailing the improbable in hopes of turning the inconceivable into the practicable. In the end, I am not sure we have done anyone a great service. In fact, I think it is counterproductive. This goes to the very heart of the question, "Why don't we invest in the creation of student leaders?" The answer is simple: WE DON'T WANT LEADERS, WE WANT FOLLOWERS. Think about it…

Sit when you are told
Play what you are told
Play when you are told
Play it the way you are told
Wear the garments you are told
Show up when you are told
Leave when you are told
Walk the way you are told

Breathe the way you are told

Breathe when you are told

Put the horn up when you are told

Put the horn down when you are told

Up bow when you are told

Down bow when you are told

Etc....

That list doesn't say leader, it says

FOLLOWER.

TRAVEL TIP

Don't believe me? At your next rehearsal try and take an individual approach to any one of these items and see whether you get positive feedback or negative feedback from your teachers and peers.

As music teachers, we bemoan the fact that our students don't display leadership qualities, and then we treat them like kindergarten students and tell them how to sit in their chairs. We wonder why they don't show more initiative and then tell them not to move when at attention. We wish they would practice more on their own, but we spoon-feed them their parts during class. It seems to me that in our heart of hearts, we don't want leaders. **We want followers who will blindly do what we say and call it leadership.** This is part of the culture we create in a highly disciplined and demanding organization. However, we are not the only ones who have faced these issues…

In recent years our military has experienced unfortunate issues relating to conduct by a few misguided people who utilized dehumanizing behavior. A few isolated events during the Iraq War such as soldiers committing murder and assaulting defenseless citizens, West Point cadets sexually harassing their female classmates, and military personnel accused of prisoner abuse at Guantanamo Bay have rocked the once-steadfast pillar of leadership known as the Armed Forces. Even though these are wayward and inappropriate acts by an isolated few, it has called into question the entire leadership structure of our military, including the President of the United States. As more concerning behavior comes to light, politicians and pundits alike have stood at the public pulpit and decried in their most outraged voices the lack of leadership in today's military. Really?! "Politicians and pundits" YES! "Lack of leadership in the military"-NO! Do we really think that our politicians should stand as judge and jury to people who are putting their life on the line in defense of our country?

Certainly, we can't condone the aforementioned behaviors and we know that most men and women serving in our armed forces display daily the courage and honor that most of us will never know or understand. However, we cannot be surprised by the nature and frequency of these transgressions. We invest so much in training these people in the art of death and destruction. We teach them seemingly incomprehensible ways to destroy and mutilate those who oppose us and then wonder why they don't show a higher level of respect and restraint when it comes to the value of a human life. The answer in my opinion is simple: WE TRAINED THEM NOT TO VALUE HUMAN LIFE. Not to oversimplify the problem, but it seems to me that when we create an effective human killing machine, then you are employing a value system that dehumanizes life. There is no way around that fact. In order to do what we ask of them, and to preserve their own lives, soldiers must devalue another life to some degree. Can someone be a successful soldier AND respect and value the life of his "enemy?" *CERTAINLY, but it is counterintuitive to how he is trained by the military to behave.*

PICTURE MOMENT

The vast majority of Americans serving in the military are brave and honorable people willing to lay down their life and pay the ultimate price for our safety and security. That is the true definition of leadership!

While not to the same extent, the problem with leadership in schools in similar. In order to be successful as an ensemble, musician and general student, you must be an excellent follower of the rules and regulations. This type of culture does not value free thinkers. It does not value risk takers. It does not foster initiative. It does not reward individuality. Can someone be successful in school and in an ensemble AND display the qualities of a leader? Certainly, but it is counterintuitive to how we train student musicians to behave. With this in mind, I ask these questions:

- *Do we really want leaders in our ensembles?*
- *If so, why do we not invest in that process?*
- *How much time and effort should be spent in pursuit of leadership?*
- *What are the benefits of this pursuit? What are the negatives?*

POSTCARD

Be honest – have you ever thought of working with the low brass as deserving of combat pay?

All jokes aside, what is the most difficult section in our group and why?

There must be a reason. What is it and how can you solve it?

This epiphany of how we may be incorrectly training or not training our students became glaringly apparent to me after a mishap on a trip many years ago. This single event was a turning point in my career as it made me realize it was not the rules that I wrote but the culture I created that was responsible for the mishap. During a long planned activity trip, one student made the unfortunate decision to bring alcohol. After we had been away from home for two days, one of my students confronted me with the rumor that someone had brought alcohol on the trip. After narrowing down the speculation as to what was fact and what was fiction through countless student interviews, which wasted a good portion of the day, we found the rumor to be true and confronted the student and her suitemates. The ladies in her room were aware that the substance was present but did not come forward with the information, nor did they correct the situation themselves.

CAR GAME

Ever heard the expression, "ignorance is bliss"? Would you rather not know if something is going wrong with your group?

What issues should cross the teacher's desk and what should be handled by students?

What should be done proactively so as to avoid these situations before they happen?

Could the example of what happened to me have been avoided? If so, how?

When I called the student's father and told him to come pick her up (he was within driving distance), he stated that he was too busy and was unable to do so. I explained to him the severity of the situation and told him I would allow him one half hour to make arrangements for his daughter's transportation home and that I would call him back to facilitate her safe return home. When I called him back thirty minutes later, he said, "Mr. Lang, I am not going to pick my daughter up and furthermore, I have reviewed your handbook and have not found any regulations that state that a student cannot have alcohol on a trip." Needless to say, I was **stunned and shocked** – instead of sharing my outrage and concern, he was tacitly endorsing his daughter's behavior, as if not having a rule against something made it acceptable. Fortunately, I am fairly quick on my feet and responded, "Sir, it does not state that I cannot leave your child at the bus station either; does that make it okay? It does not say that students cannot bring a gun on the trip; does that make it okay? As I recall, it mentions nothing about committing major felonies while on the trip; are you seriously telling me that these are also behaviors you would condone?" He was speechless. He arrived shortly thereafter to pick his daughter up.

After recovering from the initial shock (and the snickers from other teachers and frustration of the students in the program), I set out to "fix" the problem. I spent the next few months contemplating how, even after training my students in leadership, such a situation could have occurred. I re-read my program handbook – which was thorough by even the most stringent standards – to see what else I had missed and I came to the conclusion that the document needed not to be more inclusive, but less so. There is no possible way in which you can conceive of every possible scenario that one hundred-plus teenagers can create. Beyond that, why would you want to spend your time and energy focusing on those behaviors?

My professional and personal soul-searching led me to the simple conclusion that I had spent too much time creating a **class** instead of a **culture**. My students were focused on the smaller picture of rules and regulations rather than the broader scope of being a person of character.

A new year and a change of schools allowed me to reinvent myself both personally and professionally. The once-hefty, eight-page rule portion of my handbook was replaced with one simple statement: *FIRST CLASS*.

I was amazed at how quickly the theme took off and how applicable the motto was to almost any situation, from behavior to performance. We talked about the belief system almost every single day. Whether it was dealing with a performance or a behavioral issue, the motto seemed to be equally appropriate. It was a one-size-fits-all approach that allowed me a quick and easy way to remind students of the standards to which we held ourselves. The reminder was equally powerful for me.

TRAVEL TIP

Why is it that people pay so much to travel in first class? After all, they get there at the same time as the coach class passengers. They are on the same plane. The service is not THAT much better and honestly, while the food and drinks are free, you can't eat or drink that much in one trip. Why? The answer: CULTURE. Even though the end result is the same, first class offers a different experience. Which is more important to you, the end result of your group or the travel experience? Maybe you are destined for first class yourself!

While it may be difficult to quantify the term "first class," we most certainly know it when we see it and can make decisions based on that credo.

It is important to have your group's value system identified in simple terms. What worked for my group may not work for yours. You are an individual organization that serves a specific school community. Build a cultural value system that is honest, authentic and can be enforced by the director and the student leaders.

If you are trying to live by the rules, you are creating a class that is forever stuck in reaction mode. If you are a group that embraces a commonly-held set of accepted values, you are a culture that is building to the future.

Which are you – a class or a culture?

KEEP IT SIMPLE

Go back to the one page version of your group's handbook and try and create a simple motto or slogan that can be remembered and branded as a part of your program. After all, when a young person is faced with a difficult decision, is it easier to remember page 64 of the handbook or your group's credo? After you have created it, try and apply it to a variety of real-life situations and see if it works. You may just have the new first page (or only page) of your group's handbook.

My Road Map

As you will come to find, this book is about you and your group. While I may share some stories and personal thoughts, in large part this book is designed to lead you down your individual path of self-discovery. When it comes to leadership, I am not a believer in platitudes, nor do I believe that there are simple answers to complex questions. With that stated, I do think it fair to give you a simple framework (or *roadmap*) of my belief system to help you understand my thought process.

Sharing this with you is not meant to unduly influence you and in no way should be considered an endorsement as to what you should believe. As I have previously said, leadership is as much about finding a good fit for a group as it is a given set of skills and techniques. With that stated, you have the right to know in a direct manner if my beliefs regarding leadership are a good fit for your group. In each case, you will have the opportunity to explore each idea in greater depth later in the book. This list is in no way meant to be all-inclusive or an end-all/be-all document on being a good leader. Think of this list as the concrete foundation to a very large leadership house that we are about to build. Be sure to inspect the foundation and the land it is built on very carefully to see that it meets with your approval. Otherwise, your "leadership house" is liable to come crashing down at some point in the future. Time spent now will save heartache, anger and frustration in the future, for you and everyone else.

The following are the beliefs upon which I have built my house:

I BELIEVE THAT LEADERSHIP IS SITUATIONAL

In order for a leader to be successful there must be an appropriate fit amongst the needs of group, its culture, and their leadership skills and style. Just as every person is different, so is every leadership scenario. There are no magic steps to success, nor are there any simple formulas for greatness. Each scenario presents different personal challenges, circumstances, obstacles and opportunities within different organizational cultures. Even if every scenario were equal, the organizational values you represent are not, therefore will require different skills for success. As you will read later, Abraham Lincoln was wildly unsuccessful in many leadership situations before ascending to the Presidency of the United States, where his success was well-documented. In light of his overall track record, should we view him as a failed leader? Certainly not! I believe that his leadership roles did not match the value systems and challenges of his previous organizations. Even great leaders experience failure in organizations that are not a good fit for them.

TRAVEL ADVISORY

My first date with my wife was a TOTAL disaster that ended in an argument. Ten years later, we met again, fell in love and were married shortly thereafter. What changed? Did she? Did I? Was it the environment? Probably a mixture of all three.

I BELIEVE THAT ANYONE CAN LEAD

Other than intelligence, there are few characteristics that would be considered absolutes or pre-qualifiers for leadership that cannot be learned. What some may consider a leadership shortcoming, others may consider an advantage. As I stated, other than intelligence, virtually any skill one might associate in a positive way with leadership can be developed with time and energy. The question is, "Does your leadership style match the organization?" If not, how much time and energy should be devoted to making it work? The only other option is simply choosing not to be a leader. While it may be en vogue to be a member of the leadership experience, it is unrealistic to believe that everyone will be equally successful in this organization. In determining your likelihood for success, a good question to ask yourself is this: "Do my strongest talents help minimize the group's weaknesses, with little if any negative impact on the people involved?"

I BELIEVE THAT TRUE LEADERSHIP STANDS IN CONTRAST TO PERSONAL GAIN

Like it or not, we are all genetically wired for self-preservation. In the beginning and end our first reaction will always be rooted in self-interest. This does not mean that this is the best choice, but it will be your first. I don't know about you, but my first answer is almost always the wrong one. Only after true reflection do I come up with my best answer. This period of introspection gives me the perspective and distance I need to make the right choice. It is okay and even natural to think of oneself first. Darwin called this "survival of the fittest." I believe that as you climb the pyramid of success, you incur a proportional responsibility for the well-being of those beneath you. Education and experience will directly affect your ability to make correct choices and these predicators are universally accessible to everyone. It is imperative to use your knowledge and experience to better the lives of others. Remember, you can be successful without being a leader and you can be a leader without success.

TRAVEL TIP

You can lead as a performer, you can lead through service – just make sure that you are honest about which type of leader you are and which type your group needs. Be an example of that type of leader.

I BELIEVE THAT STUDENT LEADERSHIP WILL MAKE EVERYONE A BETTER PERSON, BUT NOT EVERY STUDENT SHOULD BE A LEADER

Music should be a place where everyone can grow and learn. In music, there are a multitude of opportunities for you to develop a wide variety of skills in group and individual settings. It also has the added benefit of allowing you to learn at your own pace and focusing on an area of interest of your choosing. I believe strongly that participation in a leadership program will teach skills that may not be learned from any other pursuits. With these added benefits come added responsibilities. Those not willing to shoulder their fair share of responsibility, leadership and otherwise, should not participate in the leadership program. There is simply too much at stake.

I BELIEVE THAT THE MORE YOU GIVE, THE MORE YOU WILL GET

This is not a new concept and has stood the test of time for thousands of years. Note that I used the future tense when it comes to "getting." You have to give first. Only after giving will you receive. I would even go so far as to suggest that there is a progressive level of return which serves as a multiple, based on how much you give. If you give ten percent more effort, you will get a substantially larger return. Oftentimes, people will look at what someone has and then try to make guesses as to how much that person gives in life. I prefer to look at what you are willing to give first, then I know exactly what you will get from the activity and we can then decide whether this is an appropriate position for you. **There is nothing wrong with being a "passenger" in the group, unwilling to assume responsibility. Just make sure that you do not get behind the wheel and put others at peril.**

I BELIEVE THAT IF YOU CAN, YOU MUST

Whether as a result of genetics or environment, we all have a different set of skills and talents. To underutilize them – or worse yet, fail to utilize them – is a wasted opportunity. Simply put, there is a correlating responsibility between your individual assets and the group responsibility you incur. **You need not rise to the expectations of someone else and you need not wish for skill sets you do not possess; you need only to use what you have to serve others to your very best ability.** With time and education, as your skill sets grow, so will your responsibility to use them for the good of others. To fail at this simply means to fail at being an individual. You are a spectacular and unique person, so to inhabit your life among the masses of mediocrity is to fail yourself. In the end, serving others is serving your true self.

I BELIEVE THAT TRUE LEADERS THINK WIN/WIN

It is only natural to want to be good at something. Success and its sweet rewards are not just fruits of your labor; they are a part of the fabric of the human soul. We all want to be good at something. The question is this: does our success stand in the way of someone else's? I believe that true leaders understand that their success does not need to eclipse someone else's success. There can be more than one great solo. There can be more than one great leader. There can be more than one way to teach a technique. There can be more than one great show. Finding flaws or faults with others does not make you more successful. On the contrary, it shows a deeper need not for success, but for winning. Winning and being successful are not the same thing. **Winning is a self-limiting behavior, as you are only doing just enough to be better than someone else, instead of striving to be the best that you can be.**

As I said, my list is only meant to help frame the discussion of leadership and ensure that you understand the foundation the book is built on. Also, these are my beliefs, and should in no way compel you to believe the same unless you are so inclined. In fact, I am confident that your list would look somewhat different than mine and provide things to think about. You are actually about to begin the process of creating your own list, so you may begin thinking about what you would and would not include in it.

Now you know what I believe, it is time to start thinking about what you believe. I just thought it only fair that before we start on our leadership journey together, you knew a little bit about the philosophies of your travel guide.

Taking Pictures: Understanding Point of Focus

My brother is always yelling at me about the pictures I take. He says that scenery, while nice, is a waste of film and that no one wants to see pictures of an inanimate object. Furthermore, when taking a picture with people, he prefers to crop out everything but the people and take the picture so close so that you can tell if the participants have used their nose hair trimmers recently. I disagree. I think that people become more meaningful when placed in the context of the moment: holidays, family vacations, weddings, funerals, etc.... *I think sometimes the big picture of **where** we are, is more important than **who** we are.* I think that there is a reason that the zoom lens appears on a camera and that it works BOTH ways, in and out.

In photography we are always looking for ways to get closer – more zoom, bigger screen, more mega-pixels. Life operates in much the same way as do your classes. We want to examine things from a microscopic level and analyze the most minute details to a point of boredom. Think about the painstaking detail of each and every rehearsal. Think about how many times you do something in search of perfection. Why do we do this? Why is this important? We do this based on our point of focus, what we find to be the most important element of the picture. Simply put, my brother and I do not share the same point of focus. He is focused on content where I am focused on context. He zooms in only on what is relevant to his life while I choose to focus on the life experience itself. He is not right and I am not wrong, we are just different in our approach to photography and our objectives.

Think of it this way – most of you can explain in painful detail the conflicts in your family (immediate), with great expertise the tensions of your high school (local), with some knowledge the tensions in your city (communal), with minimal eloquence the challenges of our country (culture) but could not even locate most countries in the Middle East (global). This does not make you a bad person. Like most people, you have a greater understanding of the things that are closest to you. And like most people, you probably address them with the greatest sense of importance because of their proximity rather than their significance. We as a culture confuse proximity with importance. We assume that because it is closer to us that it must have a greater impact on our life. More immediate yes, but greater? Possibly not! ***Simply stated, you do this because it is within your domain of control and realm of responsibility.***

Can you imagine doing everything with that kind of myopic approach? How would you eat a bowl of cereal? How would you watch TV when all you could see are the facial pores of the actors? How would you walk when instead of seeing what lies ahead, you could only see the T-shirt stains of the person in front of you?

CAR GAME

Are you naturally better at viewing the big picture or the finite details? Are you someone who dreams the dream or someone who makes the dream work? Do you relish or relinquish the small and necessary details that ensure success? Both types are necessary in a group. Which are you? What is your point of focus?

Take the focus to the opposite extreme with an expensive, wide-angle telephoto lens. Do you think that if you saw the world from this perspective, you would talk to people in a louder voice, since they would appear to be further away? Think about it – from your new perspective, everyone would be so far removed, you would have to shout to get their attention.

The old adage states that there are three sides to every situation: your perspective, their perspective and the real perspective. A similar notion can be said for leadership. There are three perspectives: nearsighted, farsighted and the real perspective. In finding our boundaries, we examined the farsighted perspective; now it is time to examine the other end of the spectrum: the nearsighted one.

TRAVEL ADVISORY

How often do you second-guess your fellow leaders or your teacher?

Do you make a habit of telling others how you would have done things differently?

How is this productive or helpful?

Before sharing your thoughts with others, make sure you share it with the person you are questioning first. Not only will this keep your ego in check, but it is common courtesy as well.

We all would like to think that we have a keen understanding and awareness of our point of focus and our belief systems. It is not as simple as one might think. The ability, when presented with challenges and opportunities, to clearly see all points of focus and make decisions accordingly is no small task. As a society, we like to play armchair quarterback and use 20/20 hindsight to second-guess the decisions and actions of others. Leadership books are as good at this as anyone. As you will soon read in the chapter about Michael Jordan, we have made an art form out of dissecting the decisions made by others and then letting the world know how we might have done them differently and/or better. As color commentators on life, we have the added benefit of knowing the end result prior to evaluating the process. Only after do we backtrack, analyze and decide how the situation should have been handled as opposed to how it was handled are we willing to share our thoughts. **Guess what – in leadership and in life, there is no TIVO. We can't "pause" things and fast-forward them to see how they end before we make a decision.** We have to gather as much information as we can, adjust our point of focus correctly and make a decision. There will be plenty of people willing to point out how it should have been done when it is all over.

Don't get me wrong – we *should* study past decisions; 20/20 hindsight can be a useful tool in predicting the future. However, past successes do not guarantee future ones, even when the circumstances are similar. Nor do they ensure that you will always make a decision in accordance with your value system. Only after careful consideration of ALL the issues and getting everyone in your leadership team to the same point of focus as it relates to you and your group's value system can you make an informed decision. (Notice I did not say "right" decision; as often, there are no "right" decisions.)

Should we allocate more money and resources to one part of the group over another? Should we hire another percussion instructor or another woodwind instructor?

Neither decision is wrong, as they are both valid and important needs. I would expect that, based on their point of focus, the members feel differently about the desired outcome. It is difficult to adjust your point of focus when it is directed further away from you, but **a difficult decision often involves choosing between the lesser of two evils or putting the needs of one person above another**. These are not simple or easy choices to make. They are complex and involve a wide range of issues that will often leave one or more of the parties involved hurt, frustrated, or angry. **These are the decisions of leadership.** These are the decisions that will cause you the most angst and frustration. This is where you have to rely on your best judgment, individual value system and point of focus to guide you through the process.

In this chapter, you will be making a list of your beliefs as they relate to your group. This activity is meant to assist you in preparing for situations such as those described above. By causing you to reflect on what your belief system is, this list will help you lay a foundation now for decision-making later. This will not serve as a magic checklist for decision-making but will serve as a framework for the process. As with everything else in this book, there are no right or wrong answers, just your answers. These answers will change with time, experience and knowledge. It should be a fluid list that will evolve with you. The more time you spend with it, the more closely it will reflect who you truly are.

Think about your point of focus as you answer the following question as they relate to your group. Each statement should yield at least five beliefs. I would recommend allowing a predetermined amount of time for each portion and writing as quickly and as much as possible in that time frame. One minute is a good bench mark and will allow you to complete all questions in about ten minutes. Don't judge your answers, don't even think, just write as much as possible in the one minute. This is called stream of consciousness writing and should yield some interesting results. Do this as an individual but be prepared to share your views with others and have a lively discussion.

WHAT I BELIEVE

Answer each question below based on the perspective described. Put yourself in various shoes and attempt to walk a mile in them to see if they still fit. Lets start from smallest to biggest, I recommend five brief answers to each question. Try not to spend too much time on any given one, but respond with your first thoughts.

As an individual member of this group I believe:

As a male/female I believe:

As a freshman/sophomore/junior/senior, I believe:

As a member of my section I believe:

As a student leader, I believe:

As a band member, I believe:

As a member of this school I believe:

As someone involved in public education in America I believe:

As a resident of _____ city/state I believe:

As an American I believe:

As a member of the human race I believe:

When you are done with your list, re-read them in reverse order. See how your individual beliefs pale in comparison to those of the human race or as an American citizen. The questions were the same for each segment, I just changed the point of

TRAVEL ADVISORY

Do you know what your point of focus is? Should it be adjusted? Think about this before moving forward in the book.

focus from you to something larger. Do you see how changing your zoom and point of focus altered your perspective and thus your answers? Are you making decisions with the proper point of focus or are you myopic in your approach? Do you make decisions that are best for you, best for your section, best for your ensemble, best for your school or best for music education as an entity? The same problem may yield different answers when viewed from a different point of focus. Keep in mind that as your place in your organization grows and changes, so should your point of focus. A new member of your group needs to be focused on just themselves and their responsibilities to be successful but if the leaders of your group approach things with the same point of focus, failure is sure to follow.

The important thing is that you spend some quality time reflecting on what you TRULY believe you do with the proper point of focus. There are no right or wrong answers. After you have completed the list, discussed it and exhausted your mind, take a break. Come back to the list later and see if you find any statements that you have changed your mind about or that contradict another statement contained within the same document. Don't be afraid to be bold, as the only way you can define what you believe is to take a position and see if it is right.

When sharing with others, keep your zoom on the wide setting and strive to see how your beliefs compare with others. This will take a high degree of trust but will also go a long ways toward determining what the culture of your group is.

Traveling with Boundaries

Have you ever taken a trip with someone who does not understand boundaries? Maybe they are a "close talker;" i.e.; they invade your personal space during conversations. Perhaps they think your stuff is communal stuff. Maybe they think that you are available as a human pillow, or they are content to talk your ear off about their prize-winning fingernail clippings art project for the eight-hour bus ride. Maybe their definition of unpacking means a bomb went off in their suitcase and everything is everywhere. At any rate, a perfectly good and well-planned trip can go seriously wrong just by choosing the wrong travel companion.

PICTURE MOMENT

What kind of travel companion are you?

Do you think of others in your actions?

What kind of leadership travel companion are you?

It is important to define leadership as it relates to your individual value system. In order to do this, you must have a clear understanding of what you believe and the boundaries that guide your belief system. You are an individual unlike any other, with thoughts, feelings, and dreams that are special and personal. Therefore, you should be afforded a set of rules that apply only to you. These rules are not set in concrete but are always changing as you evolve. My boundaries have changed as my life has changed and will continue to do so for as long as I inhabit this earth. While your list of beliefs may contain some commonly held attitudes, it should also be uniquely yours. These beliefs should provide a constant barometer of what it is that you aspire to be.

When creating your list, you do not need to worry about being correct. You don't need to stick to a prescribed number of statements. They do not need to make sense to anyone but you. They are yours and yours alone and should reflect the individual that you are. Your goal should be to create a set of beliefs that can guide, direct and influence you as you come across the many challenges you will face as a student leader. To start with, keep the rules simple and short so you can easily understand and abide by them.

Listed below is a set of beliefs I created. While somewhat humorous and glib (which reflects who I am), they are all rooted in a deep system of beliefs that guide me to this day. I am not always successful in living up to the values they embody, but it does give me something to shoot for. Here they are for you to read:

SCOTT'S TRAVEL LAWS

Don't teach children to say they're sorry. Teach them to avoid doing things that would require an apology.

Nothing is black and white. If they were, these colors would appear in the rainbow.

Listening is the best communication skill.

Always remember to come to the aid of the wounded, regardless of the wound. And remember that laughter is the best medicine.

Like a boomerang, everything you throw out there will come back to you. The harder you throw, the tougher it is to catch.

Surround yourself with people smarter than you. To be the Einstein among idiots is no honor.

Most truisms are not.

Always volunteer, regardless of the task.

It's impossible to lie to yourself. Make sure, however, that you are really asking the right questions.

Be willing to make a fool of yourself. It keeps the ego in check.

The more you give, the more you get.

LIST YOUR BELIEFS

Sit down and make a list of your beliefs. The list should reflect you and your personal thoughts and can be as long or as short as you would like it to be. If you are creative, you may fashion your list into a poem, a song or other work of art. The context can be just as original as the content. When everyone is done creating their lists, share them. Remember not to judge. This is not a time to try and outdo your friends or appear clever; this is a time for honesty and integrity.

Once you have shared your individual lists, see if you can create together another list that is applicable to the entire organization. The list should reflect what is important to your organization and should provide for some interesting conversation. There may be three things or thirteen things on your list. It may or may not have a theme. Just be sure to come to closure on something you can all agree to live with, as live with it you shall.

When finished, you should have the makings of something that would resemble a good mission statement for your group. You can use it word for word or create a new statement that reflects the general belief structure of the group. If the statement has more than one stated belief, then these beliefs should appear in the statement in order of importance. This will help to clarify and display for one and all the doctrine or philosophy of how your organization operates and what its priorities are. You may even want to continue the exercise with something creative like creating a group logo or crest.

CREATE A LOGO

Design a logo that reflects your group – as you would like it to be; not necessarily in its present state. Consider this design process to be a visual reminder for everyone of your chosen destination. If you already have a logo, you may choose to design a new one or embellish/improve on the old one. Be creative, clever and colorful. Seize this as an opportunity to have some fun while inspiring the members of your group. When everyone is done, tear out these sheets and tape them up for everyone to see. Either choose a single logo or combine elements from multiple logos to create a new look for your band. Sketch your ideas in the space below.

PACKING LIST

List three or more things you learned about what you believe:

How were your beliefs different from what you thought they would be?

How were your beliefs different from your peers?

After this unit, are you better prepared to be a trip planner or leadership tour guide for the trip participants in your group? How so?

PACKING LIST cont'd

What are some of the lies you believed about being a leader that you now know are not true?

Do you have all of your travel documents (notes/activities from this chapter)? If not, what documents are you lacking (list activities you did not do here, so you can come back another time and work on them)?

✳ TRAVELOGUE

CHAPTER THREE
Traveling Alone, Leading Within

"It is not the critic who counts; not the man who points out how the strong man stumbles or where the doer of deeds could have done better. The credit belongs to the man who is actually in the arena, whose face is marred by dust and sweat and blood, who strives valiantly, who errs and comes up short again and again, because there is no effort without error or shortcoming, but who knows the great enthusiasms, the great devotions, who spends himself for a worthy cause; who, at the best, knows, in the end, the triumph of high achievement, and who, at the worst, if he fails, at least he fails while daring greatly, so that his place shall never be with those cold and timid souls who knew neither victory nor defeat."

Theodore Roosevelt

"Citizenship in a Republic"

Speech at the Sorbonne, Paris, April 23, 1910

The Critic

At the end of her high school experience, a former student of mine gave me this quote. She shared with me how during her junior year, I had told her that I thought she was overly critical of people. Upset and affected by my comment, she found this quote, taped it to the mirror in her bedroom and read it every day as she got ready for school. The week of her high school graduation, she returned the quote to me and shared with me the story of how she had used it to better herself during the past two years. I framed it and hung it in my office for years as I believe that I often suffer from the same affliction. She was willing (well, mostly willing) to accept my criticism, determine its value and act upon it to better herself.

Do you have a personal or leadership flaw that you feel needs some effort and attention? Is there some element of your persona that is less than desirable? If you were to ask some of your leadership travel companions for help in bettering yourself, what would they want you to work on? Take some time and find a quote that inspires you to better yourself. You may already have one or you may need to spend some time researching. There are several books and Web sites dedicated just to quotes that can be viewed by author, content or context.

TRAVEL TIP

Sometimes, those around you will see things differently than you do. It's not a bad thing to ask friends and strangers alike for ideas on self improvement. If you are too embarrassed to ask, then read about others who have sought to travel a similar path toward personal betterment. Such reading material would also be a great place to find a meaningful quote or inspirational thought.

If you would like, take some time during a meeting and have everyone share their quotes and what makes them meaningful. Others might benefit from the experience and help pave the way to self-improvement.

Print your quote on a piece of paper and post it somewhere relevant where you will see it every day. For instance, if it is music-related, place the quote on the inside door of your instrument locker or inside your instrument case. If it is family-related, tape it to the mirror in your bathroom.

The important thing is to have a daily, tangible reminder of what you are striving for. Think of this as a mini compass that you can check daily to see if you are still on course.

PICTURE MOMENT

My quote was a brief story from a Robert Fulghum book about felling trees by yelling at them. This story reminded me of the power and damage of the tone and volume of our voices. Unfortunately, copyright laws prohibit me from printing the essay here, but you can find the story and read it for yourself in Fulghum's book *All I Really Need to Know I Learned in Kindergarten.*

Traveling Alone

Remember when I wrote this as one of my beliefs earlier in the book?

I BELIEVE THAT ANYONE CAN LEAD

Other than intelligence, there are few characteristics that would be considered absolutes or pre-qualifiers for leadership that cannot be learned. What some may consider a leadership shortcoming, others may consider an advantage. As I stated, other than intelligence, virtually any skill one might associate in a positive way with leadership can be developed with time and energy. The question is, "Does your leadership style match the organization?" If not, how much time and energy should be devoted to making it work? The only other option is simply choosing not to be a leader. While it may be en vogue to be a member of the leadership experience, it is unrealistic to believe that everyone will be equally successful in this organization. In determining your likelihood for success, a good question to ask yourself is this: "Do my strongest talents help minimize the group's weakness, with little if any negative impact on the people involved?"

Everyone has a leadership style, whether they realize it or not. Many leaders mimic the behaviors they have seen work with their predecessors and peers, while others carve out a path for themselves. Most leaders are a mixture of both. Experience and education allow us the opportunity to grow with each moment.

This part of our journey is where we try and figure out a little bit more about your leadership style and how you can be of service to your group. In leadership circles, this is called "authentic leadership." This simple catch phrase speaks to the very difficult work of finding out who you are and aligning your position, beliefs and skills with the hopes of achieving your goals in the most effective way possible. This may mean that you choose to change your style or change your job, but whatever you do, it has to reflect the REAL you. **It isn't any fun trying to be someone you are not – no one wants to follow a "poser." We can all spot these people a mile away.** People will respect and follow individuals as long as they are trustworthy and honest about who they are.

Sometimes in schools, we are so consumed by putting information *in* you that we forget bring *out* of you what is already there. We are so consumed with helping you learn what we want you to learn that we forge ahead without first acknowledging that who you are and what you believe affects how you learn. Schools often fail to take advantage of students' natural skills and abilities as they simultaneously work to help them to develop new ones. Anyone who has ever met me knows that my tenure on the varsity football team would be short-lived at best (literally short-lived, as I would be killed by the first lineman to hit me). You would also know that my only hope of dunking a basketball is a pair of stilts or a trampoline. No coach in his right mind would think otherwise in trying to put together a team, not just because the team would not win, but because I do not possess the knowledge or skills required to be successful at these tasks. More importantly, nor do I have the desire. Teachers in performance situations understand that success occurs when there is a marriage between what already is known and what can be taught. Regular classroom teachers and administrators are not as quick to assess and then align curricula and instruction to the people receiving it. Problems occur when schools ask for behaviors that are contradictory to the underlying values that are already within you. Does your school teach college prep materials to at-risk students? Does your school teach keyboarding to kids who have been on a computer since they were two? Does your school tout academics but only hold assemblies for athletics? Contradictory values such as these could cause confusion about the authentic message of what we are trying to achieve, raising the level of frustration and slowing the progress of everyone involved. Think of it as putting a Windows systems disc into an Apple computer or vice versa. They are both equally valid and amazingly complex operating systems that can achieve tremendous results, but only when used in an environment that aligns with their core values.

PICTURE MOMENT

"Are you a PC or Mac person?" has become the hip question of the new millennium. While seemingly different, the crossover is far greater than what separates them. Just ask any PC user with an iPod or any Apple user with Microsoft Office. What does the type of computer you use say about you?

This chapter is designed to help you get a better understanding of what kind of person you are and what your leadership style is. This is important because before you can lead a group, you first have to understand what kind of leader you are and what you believe. When you are able to be consistent and clear about this and find a job within your group that aligns with this style, you are far more likely to be successful and happy in all of your pursuits. So, let's get to work on finding out who you are as a leader.

Traveling Through Time: Abraham Lincoln

If I could travel anywhere, I would travel through time. I am fascinated by history and all of the lessons it can teach us. I am also deeply fascinated by history makers – what they accomplished and how they went about it. I think there are so many wonderful lessons to be learned from the past. You know the old saying from George Santayana: "Those who do not study history are doomed to repeat it." I do believe there is some truth to that. I have always said that if I could not teach music, I would have taught history – not for its dates and events, but for its stories of people and their struggles to overcome obstacles and achieve significance with their lives. Like all history buffs, I have some favorites I would like to meet in my travels. Abraham Lincoln is one of these individuals.

CAR GAME

If you could travel through time, excluding religious figures, who would you want to meet and why?

What does that choice say about your leadership style?

Few people will hear the name Abraham Lincoln and not reflect on the amazing accomplishments of his life and presidential tenure. Besides his distinct physical characteristics, his ability to succinctly and successfully speak to a nation eloquently also helped to identify him as one of the most impressive figures to have ever held this high office.

The Lincoln-Douglas Debates and the deliveries of the Emancipation Proclamation and the Gettysburg Address are events that have shaped the destination of this country forever. In addition, Lincoln led this country through what was unquestionably its most horrific and traumatic time, the Civil War – a time when brother fought against brother, father against son and the very fabric of this young nation was torn in half. There were no simple solutions to this conflict. Lincoln had to face some of the most difficult decisions ever to have faced our chief executive. Choosing abolition over national harmony still serves as the measuring stick by which all other chief executives will be judged. In a more mundane but equally important light, would you have walked a mile to return a penny, as Lincoln is said to have done?

PICTURE MOMENT

The great orators of history have always been known as impressive statesmen – Jefferson, Lincoln, Roosevelt, Kennedy and Clinton are just some of the Presidents who used the power of words to inspire and motivate. Are you a good speaker? Is this something you could use to motivate your fellow students?

In addition to being one of our greatest statesmen, Lincoln was a man of vision. Although seemingly lost among his storied accomplishments, perhaps his greatest and most wide-reaching legacy is not viewable from the battlefield at Gettysburg or the National Archives where his many documents are stored, but at the offices of the Internal Revenue Service.

Few people are aware of the fact that Lincoln was a chief architect of our current policy regarding the taxation of a citizenry. Abraham Lincoln was among the original authors of the progressive tax system. Since its inception, it has been one of the greatest sources of controversy for every Presidential administration since the 1860's. For those of you who are unfamiliar with the concept, the philosophy of the progressive tax code suggests that the more money you make, the more money you should have to pay. For instance:

If you make $200,000 per annum, you might pay $40,000 a year in federal income tax.

If you make $20,000 per annum, you might pay $4,000 in federal income tax.

If you make $2,000.00 per annum, the government actually pays you $4,000 per annum in entitlements.

Entitlements and government subsidies such as welfare, food stamps, unemployment insurance, etc. are a way of ensuring that the poorest of our citizenry are able to meet the most basic of needs, regardless of whether or not they pay taxes. Despite popular opinion and the abundance of loopholes, the top one percent of the United States' population actually pays thirty-four percent of the nation's federal taxes. The top five percent pays fifty-three percent of the nation's taxes. Simply put, those who make the most pay the most, just as Lincoln had intended.

CAR GAME

Does your group have some sort of entitlements?

Do you build in costs/fees for those that who afford them to help those who can't?

At first glance, the glaring inequities of the sliding tax scale seem quite obvious. Think about it: those who make $200,000 per annum get the same water, the same fire trucks, the same national defense system, the same streets, the same standards for meat inspection, the same postal service, etc. as those who make less. In fact, when you examine things more closely, you will find that those who pay less in taxes actually receive more services and benefits than those who pay substantially more. Typically speaking, we station more police in areas that have a lower household income – people who live in pricey gated communities have less of a need for police protection. Also, houses with fire sprinklers and state-of-the-art construction are less likely to require a visit from the local fire department. Greater access to public facilities and services tends to exist in areas where people make less money so they can have greater access to special programs and services. How can this be fair? How can this system have stood the test of time? After all, there are no other countries in the world that use this system to the extent that we do. Is this benevolence, malevolence or just plain stupidity?

Abraham Lincoln believed that those who had greater resources should bear the burden of responsibility for those who do not share in their fortunes. He believed that if you had the ability to give to a greater

> ## TRAVEL ADVISORY
>
> As you evolve, both personally and as a leader, so should what is required of you. If you can help more, you must.

extent, then you should. Simply stated (in my words, not his), **IF YOU CAN, YOU MUST. Your requirement to give should be based on your ability to give.** As your abilities change and grow, so should your responsibilities. If you can provide for those in need, you must. If you can help your section members and fellow leaders, YOU MUST!

If you think about it, it just makes sense on so many levels. We require a four-year-old to pick up her toys while the infant has her every need attended to. The eight-year-old may have to only clean his room while the teenager is expected to perform a variety of household tasks that can require physical and mental acuity. We ask a high school student to do more homework than a grade-school student. We ask AP/honors students to do more work than students with less intellectual ability, even though they get the same high school diploma. Does this meet the standards of equity for all? Should this merit further study and scrutiny? Why should you get the same diploma if you did significantly more work? Well, you can thank Abraham Lincoln, among others, for that.

We have created a culture in America that says that the more you can offer, the more you HAVE to offer. Your requirements and responsibilities are based upon your abilities and opportunities. As I said previously, **IF YOU CAN, YOU MUST.**

If this same standard was brought to bear on leadership, it would imply that whatever you can do to help the organization, you must. Your commitment to give is not based on your desires so much as it is based on needs and opportunities. Those who have more opportunities have more responsibility. Since leadership provides more opportunities, then it also bears the burden of greater responsibilities. Having said that, here are just a few examples for you to consider:

- If you can march perfectly, then you must, because there are those who can't walk.
- If you can practice, then you must, because there are those who can't play an instrument.
- If you can clean your facility, then you must, because there are those who have no music rooms.
- If you can help another student musician, then you must, because there are those who have less talent than you.
- If you can make music, then you must, as there are special needs students who will never know the joy of playing Mozart.
- If you can be involved in your school, then you must, as there are students your age in other countries that have no schools.
- If you can love another human being, you must, because there are those who have no love.

This list is certainly not meant to be all-inclusive, but should serve as an opportunity to start your own list. Each individual's list of what they can give should be different as their ability to give is different. No two people are the same; therefore no two lists are the same. This is not a chance to list a few of the things you would *like* to do, but a chance to list everything that you are *going* to do. No detail is too minute. No task is too small. List EVERYTHING! Each sentence should look like this:

Because I can _____ **then I must** _____.

TRAVEL TIP

Strive to fill two full pages with these. One page should be technical skills (cleaning, fixing, writing, etc...), one page should be life skills (smiling, being polite, greeting by name, etc...).

If you have time, the list can go on and on. You are blessed with a multitude of talents, skills and abilities that are special to you. Whether they are genetic, physical or mental, the end result does not change: **IF YOU CAN YOU MUST, BECAUSE THERE ARE THOSE WHO CAN'T**; and to squander it would be irresponsible and inexcusable.

But I am busy. But I am tired. But I already work hard enough. But there is not enough time in the day. We all face obstacles, both real and perceived, which inhibit us from reaching the heights we were truly meant to achieve. It is only when we remove the excuses and exceptions that we can truly rise and see ourselves for who we REALLY are.

Let's get back to Abraham Lincoln. Few people remember that he was defeated eight times before finally being elected to his first public office. He had similar results during the rest of his life prior to becoming President. For instance, he entered the Blackhawk War as a captain, yet was demoted to private by the end of the war. In addition to this:

> *At age 22...failed in business*
>
> *At age 23...was defeated for the state legislature*
>
> *At age 25...failed in business again*
>
> *At age 26...coped with the death of his sweetheart*
>
> *At age 27...suffered a nervous breakdown*
>
> *At age 29...was defeated for speaker of the Illinois House*
>
> *At age 34...was defeated for congressional nomination*
>
> *At age 37...was elected to Congress*
>
> *At age 39...lost re-nomination for Congress*
>
> *At age 46...was defeated for the Senate*
>
> *At age 47...was defeated for the vice-presidency of the U.S.*
>
> *At age 49...was defeated for the Senate again*
>
> *BUT...at age 51, was elected President of the U.S.*

In his personal life he faced equal if not greater challenges. We know that his wife, Mary Todd Lincoln, struggled with mental illness to a degree that inhibited her ability to function on the most basic levels at times. Finally, recent examinations of Lincoln's life to an even greater extent through his own personal writings and second-party accounts suggest that Lincoln himself most likely suffered from mental illness; more specifically, depression. Given these immense setbacks and personal failures it seems unlikely that he would have risen to such great heights and achieved such substantial accomplishments. Knowing this, who better to author such a structure as the progressive tax system? Who better to challenge the American people – past, present and future – to fully discover and seek out not just their responsibilities but also their abilities? If he could, he did; *so if you can, you must*.

This approach to life expects us not only to live our lives to the fullest but challenges us to help others live their lives in an equal fashion. Because we have the ability to be a good neighbor,

> ## PICTURE MOMENT
>
> Do you use obstacles in your life as an excuse to under perform as a person and/or leader?

we must. Because we have the ability to serve other students, we must. Because we have the ability to help other music programs, we must. Because we have the good fortune of being able to raise money for those in need, we must. Because you have the ability to be a contributing member of your family, you must. The list goes on and on. Furthermore, as your abilities grow, so will your responsibilities. As you abilities diminish, so will your responsibilities. In time, when you are no longer able to care fully for yourself, someone else will care for you…because they can.

Our communities are growing larger, which means our world is growing smaller. This has never been more evident than in the recent past as our world has struggled with catastrophic losses in the recent Asian tsunami, the devastating earthquake in Pakistan and hurricane Katrina. Even in our own abundantly affluent country we have seen the aftermath of natural disasters and terrorist attacks reduce once seemingly rich and promising lives to ruin and rubble. No one is shielded from the possibility of what may come, so no one is shielded from the responsibility of what we may do to help. This is the very essence of leadership. This is the very essence of humanity.

POSTCARD

List five things that you could do but don't. The list could include studying more, practicing more, being friendlier. Choose something that you can and would like to do more of and create an action plan for achieving your goals. Remember, goals have to be specific and measurable.

1.

2.

3.

4.

5.

The Best Part of Traveling: Food

As you grow older, you learn to appreciate different things about spending time in different cultures. What entertained you at the age of eight (the world's largest ball of twine) is not what will entertain you at the age of forty-eight (I am not that old, so I am not sure what entertains people of this age). I do know however that as I have grown, so has my appreciation for the importance food plays in a successful trip. The dine and dash at Disneyland in search of the next thrill when you are young gives way to the three-hour, four-course meal during which an adult hopes to avoid any appearance of thrills. Ahhhh yes, I do enjoy a good gastronomic delight. Of course, I also LOVE the churros at Disneyland, but that addiction is another story altogether.

PICTURE MOMENT

What is your "comfort food?"

What memories does it evoke?

Can you associate major events or conversations in your life with the food you were eating at the time?

What is your favorite food smell and why?

Prior to writing one more word, I must make a confession. I am a disaster in the kitchen. I cannot tell the difference between a colander and cauliflower. My ignorance goes well beyond that of the average male who spent thirty-five bliss-filled years as a bachelor. Sure, I can do the important stuff – you know, manly things like grilling raw flesh over an open flame in a bravado display of testosterone. I can even make a mean peanut butter and jelly sandwich (super-chunky peanut butter, of course). But beyond that, I am a total waste of human space in the kitchen.

My wife (who taught a high school culinary class) has made it abundantly clear on many occasions that I am an amateur and that my skills would be better applied to other endeavors, like cleaning the garage. She minces no words and makes no bones about it. My place in the kitchen (when allowed) is relegated to stirring, slicing and cleaning up. Actually, it is mostly just cleaning up, as she is still somewhat suspect of my other two skills. I am a most excellent cleaner by any stretch of the definition.

She is a good person, and has made a yeoman's effort to educate me on some of the more essential culinary skills. However, it appears that I have no aptitude, patience, or desire to acquire them. *It is not that I don't want to KNOW how to cook; it is just that I do not want to LEARN how to cook.* They are not the same. I want the skill of a master chef without doing the work.

TRAVEL ADVISORY

Do you want to have good grades but lack the effort? Do you want to be in a great music group but fail to practice? Do you want to be a successful leader but not have to invest time and effort? This is the difference between wanting to know and being willing to learn.

I wish that I could cook. I love watching cooking shows on television. The stars of these shows make it look so easy and so much fun. When they cook, it seems so creative and exciting, but every time I cook, it seems to be none of the above. I am not sure what I am doing wrong but I always seem to be doing something wrong. They dice, slice, stir, and make flames rise out of the pan like dancing balls of light choreographed to the sizzling music of the skillet. I, too once made flames rise out of the pan. However, it was not intentional, and I had to resort to squirting a bunch of water in the pan to put it out. This is how I learned that the adage "oil and water do not mix" really does hold true.

Having noted my lack of culinary skills, I'd like to share a quick story with you. Trying to be a good husband, I recently offered my humble services to help my wife through a holiday cooking project. I was willing to do whatever lowly task needed to be done to help her complete her project. (Okay, let's be honest – there was nothing on television and I was bored. Nevertheless, I was able and willing to help.)

I have declared that I am the official stirrer in my kitchen. If there is something to be mixed or intermingled, I am the man for the job. I like this job. It keeps me busy, occupied and requires very little definable skills. Besides, on television, this is where the action is. Stirring and mixing seem to involve all the fun. Not only do you get to pulverize things, sometimes even over an open flame, but you get to add a dash of this and a pinch of that to make the creation something all your own. I never know what I am adding – parsley and parsnips all seem the same to me and I could not tell a clove of garlic from a cinnamon clove. I am not even sure that I care to. I just like the notion of creating something different – different from the recipe, something unique to me.

Since I have the unenviable combination of a cast iron stomach, a poorly developed palate and a low set of culinary expectations, I can tolerate just about anything I create. So it is with this combination of zero skills and boundless energy that I offered to assist my lovely wife.

The day's project...cookies. I LOVE COOKIES. I believe that cookies should be their own food group. I mean, there are certainly enough varieties and their ingredients encompass most of the major food groups, depending on how you make them. Besides, cookies are one of the few things I can make and eat, raw or cooked, along the way so I can hear my wife scream, "STOP THAT! DO YOU WANT TO GET FOOD POISONING AND DIE?" I love this question because she sees it as rhetorical and I see it as an opportunity to antagonize her. I smugly remind her that the cavemen ate off dirt floors and survived just fine! She responds, "YEAH, but they died in their thirties and you are closer to *forty*, so laugh it up, dead man!"

To continue, she began by sending me over to the counter to chop chocolate and break some eggs. I love breaking eggs. I always try and do it one-handed while looking cool. It rarely works out, but you know what they say – "practice makes perfect" – so I keep practicing. Once I tried to juggle eggs...well I think you know the ending to that story. Upon on the successful completion of this task, she sent me, all giddy with my success, to work the mixing bowl...YES! Power tools for the kitchen! Men love to work with power tools, even if they are wearing an apron at the time. Besides, this was a huge show of confidence in me by my wife. Not only had I graduated from the whisk and spatula, but I was being upgraded to the real expensive cooking toys. This was a big moment; my graduation day. My cooking training wheels were off and I was ready to roll.

I dumped all of the ingredients into the bowl and surveyed the assortment of speeds from which to choose. Man alive, how could there be so many options for mixing? *Stir, puree, whip, blend, crush* – as far as I'm concerned, they could have just put fast, faster, fasterer, fastererer and fastest. It would serve the same purpose. Being the efficient person that I am, I chose the highest speed. It seemed to make sense, after all. Why take minutes to accomplish what could be done in seconds? If nothing else, call me efficient! I would show my wife a thing or two and with the press of a button…WHOOOOOOOOOOOOSH!!!

After cleaning the cookie dough off of the cabinets and ceiling, I received the requisite scolding about appropriate use of kitchen equipment and paying attention to what I was doing. She threatened to ground me from use of any appliance that required electricity. I spent the better part of five minutes acting remorseful (which I wasn't) and begging for another chance (which I wanted). Soon my puppy dog eyes and persistent nagging earned me another chance to work with the power tools. Having learned from my experiences, I was more careful the second time around (at least while she was looking) and completed the task in what appeared to be a sufficient manner.

As we continued the process of baking cookies, I viewed the ingredient list more as a guideline than a requisite list. I wanted to approach the baking of cookies with the same reckless abandonment I used in cooking. It turns out that you can't do this. My patient wife explained to me that baking is a science. Unlike the freewheeling approach to cooking, baking is an exercise in following directions (something that has been proven not to be my strong point). It turns out that there is little room for creative interpretation in the world of baking. In the chemical reaction that is baking, if we fail to meet the necessary conditions or alter the size and scope of the ingredients in any way, we might not get the expected results. In a saucepan an extra pinch of salt, a little more flour and five additional minutes can be genius, but those same conditions in an oven can produce unexpected and horrible-tasting results. It made sense to me; I had just never thought of it in quite that way.

POSTCARD

Write a recipe for your leadership position:

What are the required tools?

Would you label your creation as easy, medium or advanced?

What products would be needed to complete the project?

How much time would be required?

Do you possess all of the needed ingredients?

Me? I am a cooker, a chef. I see things on an artistic level. As I get older, I have less and less of an appreciation for rigid rules and those who enforce them. I understand the need for structure and oversight, but as a leader, I prefer cooking. I prefer to see scenarios as unfinished opportunities for me to solve problems in a personal way. No two people are exactly the same; so therefore, no two situations involving people can be the same. As far as I am concerned, my approach to leadership calls for a dash of caring, a pinch of knowledge and a smidgen of strength.

I do not do well with rules and regulations. I thrive in and appreciate an atmosphere of structure. I like boundaries because they help me to understand where the lines are drawn. They provide fences that keep me from straying too far from where I need to be but give me room to roam. More importantly, they give me room to grow and learn.

I think different scenarios and different times call for different types of leaders. There is no single approach that will serve all people equally well. I believe that there are few important situations that are so clear that they provide little room for interpretation and exploration.

PICTURE MOMENT

Are you as good at following directions as you are at giving them? Do you work as hard at being an assistant as you do at being a leader? Are you willing to follow someone else's (leadership) recipe, even if you think yours is better?

There is a need for bakers – people who understand, appreciate and follow precise and specific directions. I would not want my doctor to be a chef, I would not want a fighter pilot to be a chef, and I would not want my pharmacist to be a chef. As I said, there is a distinct and ever-growing need for these people – I just know that I need not apply.

Are you a baker or a chef? Neither is better, neither is worse. Which set of skills does your position call for? Typically a music librarian would have the skill sets of a baker, while a drum major would have those of a chef. Your group treasurer should be a baker while the person who decorates the bulletin boards should be a chef.   There is no right or wrong job. There is no right or wrong person; there are just right and wrong people for the jobs. Either way, be sure to cover everything up before turning on the blender – I should know, I am still cleaning cookie dough off of our kitchen ceiling.

DISCUSSION QUESTIONS

As a leader, which are you: a baker or a chef?

What skills do you have in these areas?

What is your job in the organization?

Does your leadership job require "baking" skills or "cooking" skills?

Are you the right fit for the job for which you have been chosen?

What areas will you need to improve upon to be effective at your job?

How are you going to improve them?

Is there a master chef (leader) to guide you through the process?

Who is that person and how can you maintain contact?

RECIPE FOR SUCCESS

With another student leader, prepare a meal or treat for the next meeting. Use this as an opportunity to display your skills or learn new ones. In addition it will provide you time to talk about the group and possible areas of growth. This act of servitude will not only fill their tummies but also warm their hearts. Make sure to provide your recipe for success to your group as you dole out the treats. After all, if they are going to eat your food, they are going to have to listen to your opinion!

List your possible meal ideas and recipes below:

Traveling with Pets: The Grainger Effect

Much has been written about man's relationship with his canine counterparts, commonly known as man's best friend. (Or in my case, better described as man's only friend.) You hear and read a lot about this relationship and the sometimes extraordinary turns it can take. That is not to say that similar relationships do not occur between humans and other pets, such as snakes, Chihuahuas (closer to rats than dogs, if you ask me), birds and cats, but it is not the same. You have to mention cats, otherwise you offend a sect of multi-generational shut-ins who treat soap operas as if they were real and can knit a human likeness of Spock out of belly button lint that would even scare Jerry Springer.

CAR GAME

Although I love cats and had one as a child, can you tell that I am a "dog person" (insert slobber joke here)? Are you more comfortable around one or the other? Go around the room quickly and see who is a "cat person" and who is a "dog person" and see if there are any noticeable patterns.

The societal lines have been drawn between those who are "cat people" and those who prefer their more slobbersome counterparts, dogs. While we could spend the better part of this book arguing the merits of either, I believe that regardless of your personal preference, the benefits are the same: unconditional love, comfort and personal joy. These are the qualities we search for in our pets and our humans as well.

I ran across a study recently in which people were asked to view forty-five separate photos of dogs and their owners to see if they could pair them up in a correct match.

Study participants were shown a photo of a dog owner and were then shown a picture of two different dogs. The participants were then asked to pair the four-legged friend with their suspected two-legged partner. It turned out that people were able to do it successfully with an alarming degree of accuracy. The article stated that this could be accounted for in one of two ways:

1. *The owner selected a dog which he/she felt most resembled themselves in some physical or behavioral manifestation,*

OR

2. *Over time, the dog and the owner had somehow physically adapted to develop similar outward features.*

I realize that the second hypothesis may seem slightly implausible, especially if you are not a canine aficionado. But you may be surprised to hear that there have been studies that chronicle similar morph-like effects between couples who have been married twenty-five years or more. Yes, that's right; there is a distinct possibility that if you and your spouse are together long enough, you each will acquire some of the same physical features of the other. If this is true, either I am going to become a very attractive man or my wife is going to be one short, ugly woman.

In the study, organizers attributed the apparent similarities to owner selection more than to a physical change over the lifetime of the pet/owner relationship. On this count, I am not so sure I agree. I know these scientists have their reasons for believing what they believe, but I have my own theory. I call it the Samba vs. Grainger effect.

Samba and Grainger were two purebred Golden Retrievers given to my roommate and me some fourteen years ago. They were born of the same parents but were one litter and six months apart. Both dogs were taken from their litter at the six-week mark and were raised entirely by my roommate and me. In order for you to fully appreciate the irony of the situation, I should tell you a little bit about my former roommate.

Jon Gomez is one of the most meticulous, anal-retentive, type-A, methodical and smart people you will ever meet. He is the type of guy who really "has it together." If you were to visit his office, you would be overwhelmed by its sense of organization and structure. Everything has a place and everything is in its place. He has an impeccable sense of style that is difficult to differentiate from that of leading designers of the day. In addition, he is a warm and charming person whose intellect has been well-suited to every leadership position he has held. He has a Teflon coating that makes him seem unflappable and always knows what to say and when to say it. This isn't just my assessment; everyone who knows him would agree.

Me? Well, I am one of those people who aspire to be like Jon, but just don't seem to have the right bag of tricks. I have been described in somewhat different terms. I am more of a ready-FIRE-aim-type guy. I tend to reveal my thoughts even before I have fully evolved them and have been known on occasion to react rather than respond to a challenging conversation. I am loyal and sometimes needy, lacking a strong sense of style with an overdeveloped need for consistency and patterns and I have yet to complete an entire meal without wearing some portion of it on my shirt and/or tie. I talk to myself constantly, in part to compensate for the lack of people nearby and I am convinced that every new person I meet should be my friend. I do not, however, stick my nose in inappropriate places as a greeting. Sure, I have many wonderful characteristics, but I am not sure charm and poise are on the list of qualities that I possess. They aren't on my dog's list, either.

Grainger (my dog) has a personality that mirrors my own. We like the same foods, make the same noises, and on occasion, smell very similar. There is also the tacit understanding that neither of us is very bright. Neither of us have never been accused of being a quick study and we both know that there are those who have more going on upstairs than the two of us. In addition, there is an unspoken understanding between us of each other's moods. I forgive her occasional nose-in-the-crotch transgressions just as she forgives my occasional surprise tackles. She loves a good back scratch (as do I) and is most assuredly an attention hog (as am I). Grainger also shares my lack of poise at crucial times. In fact, she has been known to butt-sniff and lick herself inappropriately in the most disadvantageous of times. She is not shy about who she is and does not particularly care what you think about her. She is comfortable in who she is and the love I have for her and worries very little about anything else.

Samba, my roommate's dog, on the other hand is incredibly poised, refined and intelligent. She possess perfect posture and plays games only that require her to out-think her sister and not out muscle her. She knows when to bark and more importantly, whom to bark at. She is meticulously groomed and won't go into any area where there is standing water or mud, as she does not like to get her paws dirty. She eats FIRST and leaves what she chooses for her sister. She learns in minutes tricks that it takes Grainger days to learn. She is a snob and a diva in every sense of the word, and a smart one at that.

The dogs both give me what I need: love and acceptance. Both dogs require the same from me, but my relationships with them are different. Grainger is special, I think, because we are cut from the same cloth.

You could say that I picked out a dog that matched my personality – except she was a gift. You could say that my roommate picked out a dog that matched his personality – except she was a gift as well. So for me, I am going to go with the aforementioned second explanation: that we have morphed to be one. I am who I am in part because of her and she is who she is in part because of me. This thought gives me comfort. This thought gives me joy. This thought also makes me responsible to her in a way I cannot explain. I know that what I give to her will be given back to me and make me the person she wants and needs me to be: kind, caring, unconditionally loving, and loyal to the end.

Organizations and groups behave in a similar manner. Over time, people gravitate inward toward a commonly accepted set of values that define who they are and how they behave, in both personal and professional ways. What may work for IBM may not work for Google. They each have created a specific cultural identity. Part of their cultures come by choice and are openly discussed, while other parts are more elusive and are observable only after long periods of time, during which the members morph together with the organization. For instance, the dress code of shirt and tie may be what is "spoken" in the company policy manual, while "casual Friday" is an accepted phenomenon discovered after a few weeks on the job. Not all examples are this easy to point out, but you get the gist.

CAR GAME

Speaking of uniforms...the rules you have regarding the use and treatment of your group shirts and uniforms says a lot about the culture of your organization. For years, IBM required a white or blue dress shirt, tie and dark slacks, while Google would just prefer that you were not naked. What does your uniform policy say about your culture?

So why did I share this with you? I did it because I think everything in life is this way. I think that the people and things we surround ourselves with unknowingly change and bend our character in directions similar to those surroundings. Have you ever done something kind in the presence of someone kind? Have you ever acted silly in the presence of someone silly? Have you ever found yourself doing dumb things in the presence of the same kind of people time and time again? The process may be slow and unnoticeable at times, but I believe that we are all on a long and difficult journey toward being one. Whether you realize it or not, you are like a chameleon. You are constantly adjusting to your surroundings, physically, emotionally and mentally. The question is, with whom and what do you surround yourself? Me? I am just trying to be more like Grainger, so I can be more like myself.

POSTCARD

Write the name of your favorite pet here

Why do you identify with this pet more so than others?

What does that say about you?

PERSONALITY PATTERNS

Write the names of the three people you spend the most time with:

Do you see a pattern in the characteristics or qualities of these people? If so, what is it?

How are they reflected in you?

How are you reflected in them?

What is the general personality of your group?

What are the strengths and weaknesses of that personality type?

What are some positive manifestations?

What are some non-positive manifestations?

What are three tangible things your leadership group can work to change without changing the personality of your group?

Shooting Stars: The Michael Jordan Effect

Most people like to mix business travel with a little pleasure. Whenever I visit a new city, I try and find some time to see something new, do something I have never done before, or catch a little bit of the local fare. Once in a great while, I am able to treat myself to the Lombardi Trophy of travel luxuries, a professional sports event.

I have visited the city of Chicago more than ten times and I consider it one of my favorite places on the planet. It has everything – culture, museums, music, and of course, sports. To be specific, the greater Chicago area is home to professional

> ## PICTURE MOMENT
> What is your favorite place to travel to and why? Is there a city you would like to visit just to see a team play or group perform? Which one is it and why?

franchises in football, basketball, hockey, not one but TWO baseball teams, and several amateur and college teams as well. These teams don't need to compete for attention as each can claim its own legion of fans. After all, the Cubs have not won a world championship in almost a century, but they still manage to sell out EVERY game. (This is different from the teams in my city, where hardly anyone wins, and they can't give the tickets away even when they do.) The myriad of choices for entertainment in this city make it nearly impossible for the average fan like me to catch a game while on the run. In my ten visits to Chicago, I have been to the theatre, the symphony, the museums, the jazz clubs, the Second City Comedy Troupe, and so much more, and yet my real travel dream remains unfulfilled.

Chicago can also claim a few well-known names among its inhabitants, past and present. Many people would place Michael Jordan right next to Al Capone as two of Chicago's most famous citizens. They are famous for different reasons, but famous nonetheless. Beyond being Chicago's favorite son, most people would agree that Michael Jordan is one of the greatest basketball players of all time. His artistry, athleticism and congeniality have established him as a sports and pop culture icon beyond compare. To look at just a few of his many accomplishments gives us insight into his unmatched ability on the hardwood.

Career highlights include:

- Five-time NBA Most Valuable Player (1987–88, 1990–91, 1991–92, 1995–96, 1997–98)
- Ten-time All-NBA First Team selection
- A member of six Chicago Bulls NBA championship teams
- Six-time NBA Finals Most Valuable Player
- The 1987–88 NBA Defensive Player of the Year and record nine-time NBA All-Defensive First Team selection (1987–88 to 1992–93, 1995–96 to 1997–98)
- Holds the NBA record for most seasons leading the league in scoring (10)
- Shares the NBA record with Wilt Chamberlain for most consecutive seasons leading the league in scoring (seven: 1986–87 to 1992–93)
- Participated in twelve NBA All-Star Games (1985, 1987–1993, 1996–98, 2002), starting
  12 times (one game missed due to injury)
- Selected in 1996 as one of the "50 Greatest Players in NBA History"
- Named the MVP of the 1988, 1996 and 1998 NBA All-Star Games

These are just a few of Jordan's many on-court accomplishments. Believe me, the complete list of his records would make for a book of such epic proportions that it would make the dictionary seem meek in comparison. Plenty of people, including Michael Jordan himself, have chronicled his success as the round-ball phenom.

I liken leadership to the basketball stylings of Michael Jordan, not for his accomplishments, which we can see, but for what we can't see. Since his high school days, virtually every move Michael has ever made, on the court and off, has been recorded on digital video. This means that every second of his public life can be analyzed and broken down to the nanosecond on digital video. After watching these films, few people would question the idea of Jordan's artistry, athletic prowess and leadership skills as something truly exceptional. Not only is his combination of abilities both athletic and artistic incredible, but his commitment to the team process and willingness to handle the ball in clutch situations has made him an icon in all of sports history. While all of this certainly qualifies him as a leader in the eyes of most, in my opinion, this is not where his true genius lies.

As I said, we have the ability to review and analyze virtually every move Michael Jordan has made since exiting high school and suiting up with the North Carolina Tar Heels. Practically his entire career and life has been captured on film and left for history to judge. Few athletes have been more watched, photographed, analyzed, and emulated. The phrase first coined in a national ad campaign of "I want to be like Mike" became not only a successful slogan but a way of life for thousands of teenagers. Everyone sees with their own eyes what he can do with a round ball, but is that really what separates him and his accomplishments from all of the players before him?

As I said, using today's technology, it would be very easy to break down a recording of one of Jordan's games, frame by frame, and recreate his every step. We can plot out each and every critical situation, dissect it and analyze his every move. With few exceptions, we can even ask players of far less skill to reenact his every step and achieve similar results. Furthermore, we can dissect Jordan's after-game analysis and gain insight into why he made the decisions he made.

We can gain a retrospective glimpse of the processes and factors that went into the situation from his perspective. We can even delve into his psyche and view his lifetime of experiences in whole and relate them to the present day in hopes of gaining a better understanding of his genius. We can do all this and more, and yet we can't create another MJ. I say this because the true genius of Michael Jordan lies in two places we cannot see – his head and his heart.

PICTURE MOMENT

Who is your Michael Jordan?

Who do you look to as a symbol of greatness?

Who is a musician that you would like to emulate?

What separates that person from the rest?

What separates him/her from you?

What did this individual do at your age to prepare for performances?

It is not just his athletic prowess that makes him so extraordinary, but an intangible ability to analyze, assess and react to an ever-changing scenario within a fraction of a second that separates him from other athletes. Nor is it his ability to drive to the bucket, dunk with power, complete a no-look pass, release to the open spot, and drop a thirty-foot jumper as if it were a lay-up. Virtually every player in the N.B.A. has these physical skills.

Impressive, yes; genius, NO! It is his internal vision, assessment and decision-making skills that have allowed him to rise above his peers. His standards of excellence and inability to quit have established him as one of the greatest athletes of all time. As is the case with leadership, it is his actions that make the highlight reels, but it is his heart and mind that have made him a champion six times. You won't see those on digital video, but they are in you! They are in each one of us. The vehicle may be different, but each and every human being is born with passion and a single-minded sense of focus. ***The questions to ask then become, does our passion match our position? Are our vocations and visions one and the same? Are we able to create a synergy between what we do and what we love to become the best at what we are?***

So what does this mean? Bottom line, in leadership as in life, we cannot create greatness in our athletes or our leaders. I will define greatness here as the state of accomplishment that transcends training. We no more can create a great teacher, artist, scientist, author or poet than we can create another Michael Jordan, because what creates greatness is not within our control. It is within yours! There is something indescribable and magical that occurs when we are in the presence of people who operate in this upper plateau and whom we know to be different and yet indefinable. We can touch it, see it, and feel it. We can analyze it and appreciate it on many different levels; we just can't re-create it. BUT YOU CAN.

Unfortunately, millions of young people are spending hours upon hours attempting to recreate MJ's patented jump shot, when they might benefit more from spending time in a classroom developing their decision-making skills. The necessity of creating and developing technical skills is obvious, but is that all that is required for greatness? Is there not something else? Are there not other skills involved? If so, what are they and how do we develop them?

There are drills, routines and daily regimens that can ensure your physical development and success as an athlete, but what are the "off-court" drills and routines?

> **"Talent wins games, but teamwork and intelligence win championships."**
>
> *- Michael Jordan*

Without these "other skills," you might be thinking at this point, If I can't be great, why try? The answer is simple: YOU CAN BE GREAT; you just have to find out where your genius lies, and that place where talent, skill, passion and personal character combine to create something truly extraordinary. You may not know it now, but in time, with effort, you will find your place as a great friend, section leader, drum major, squad leader, parent, businessperson, politician, preacher, soldier…the list goes on and on. Beyond your genius, you can be exceptional at anything you choose. The world does not need a team of Michael Jordans to be successful. *The world needs a team of individuals who have greatness in their own right – as a trainer, dietician, sixth man, coach, general manager, marketing director, concessions coordinator and parking supervisor, for without their successes, you might never know the name Michael Jordan.* Think of it this way – without the genius of the architect, there would be no arena in which to play basketball. Without the genius of the city planner, there would be no roads to get to the stadium. Without the genius of the television producer, there would be no way for millions of people to watch Jordan play. While receiving most of the attention, Michael Jordan's genius is only one small part of the overall organizational genius. Everyone has to do their part. Remember what Michael said: *"Talent wins games, but **teamwork** and **intelligence** win championships."* Are you doing your part for your team?

Even though the parking lot attendant plays an important role, that role does lack a certain "fame quality" to it. No one is clamoring to buy his jersey. He doesn't have people begging him for his autograph. He may be the best parking attendant ever, but it is unlikely we will see his name in the stadium "Ring of Honor" or see a statue of himself at the entrance of the stadium. Yes, his life may be a little more mundane, but also a little more sane. Just remember that the fame of leadership comes at an extreme price.

People often mistake leadership for visibility. We see people on TV and sports and they become role models... what they wear and say impact culture. That does not make them leaders. Well, it does not make them good leaders. In addition to being scrutinized for his actions on the court, Jordan's personal life was dissected like few people before him. The media age that had afforded both him and his sport unparalleled access to the public and widespread success would also prove to be unforgiving, unrelenting and unnerving during times when the attention was unwelcome. This was evidenced during his hiatus from basketball, the death of his father and the end of his marriage.

CAR GAME

Have you ever worked with or for a leader that could "shine" when under the spotlight but disappeared when the real work needed to be done? How did you respond to that type of leadership?

Without speaking of anyone in your current organization, describe this person as a leader and how people responded to him or her.

There is no on/off switch to fame; the switch is permanently stuck in the on position. There is no on/off switch to leadership. Just as Michael Jordan could not choose to "ease off" on or off of the court, neither can a leader. While other players might miss a practice or take a breather on the bench, the standard of excellence to which Jordan is held does not afford him such a luxury. Off nights and bad practices are fodder for the front page when you are the greatest player on earth. Every day, every practice, every moment of your day is "game on." Are you ready for this? Are you ready for the scrutiny associated with visibility? As a leader, you are on stage at all times, being watched and mimicked whether you want to be or not. When you choose to be a leader you surrender the right to give less than your best. There is no "temporary leadership," nor are there "part-time leaders." True leaders are on call and on watch every waking moment. If you seek the glory of the solo in the show, or time on the podium, then you must be willing to accept and embrace the responsibility that accompanies it. Do you still wish you were Michael Jordan?

POSTCARD

What are the things you are most passionate about?

What are the things you enjoy doing the most?

Do you have an idea where your genius might be?

What do you need to be happy in life?

POSTCARD CONT'D

Do you thrive in climates of pressure?

Do you want the ball, the solo, the decision when everything is on the line, or do you prefer being in the background?

Do you embody the values of the organization you wish to represent?

Do you represent your organization in a manner that reflects well on the organization?

What task in your group do you think you are best suited for?

If you could do only one thing in this group, what would it be?

Are you currently in the position that best utilizes your strengths?

If not, why and what position are you better suited for? If the position does not exist, make one up!

PACKING LIST

Are you better at baking or cooking?

Explain:

How were your beliefs different from what you thought they would be?

Which was your teacher, a baker or a chef? Is this helpful or hampering? List three ways for each:

How were your skills different from your peers? Were there more bakers or cookers in your group? How would that affect you and your group?

What are some strategies you could use to combat these issues?

PACKING LIST cont'd

After this unit, how are you better prepared to be a leader in your group?

Who is the leader (or leaders) you would travel the furthest to see (both in past time and real time)?

Why?

How do you resemble them? How are you different?

What is your favorite recipe? Could you replicate it so that someone else could make it just as well, or do you "wing it" differently each time you make it? How does this compare to your leadership style?

Would you want to be Michael Jordan? If not, why?

If not MJ, is there someone else whose leadership position appeals to you?

PACKING LIST cont'd

Do you have all of your travel documents (notes/activities from this chapter)?
If not, what documents are you lacking (list activities you did not do here, so
you can come back another time and work on them)?

✴ TRAVELOGUE

CHAPTER FOUR
Traveling with a Group, Leading Throughout

I have found out that there ain't no surer way to find out

whether you like people or hate them than to travel with them.

Mark Twain

Traveling with a Group

Anyone who has traveled with a group of people knows that it is much different than traveling alone. Gone are the individual freedoms and last-minute itinerary changes. Gone are the long afternoons of lost hours and arriving just in the nick of time for your plane. The complexities of modern travel are infinitely more difficult when you add a crowd, but so are the opportunities if you plan for them. Think about it – group discounts, making new friends, shared memories and a chance to experience the dynamic of the group experience that can never be replicated single-handedly. As I said, group travel can be incredibly rewarding IF YOU PLAN FOR IT!

Each summer I taught, I would take my leaders out of town for a three-day leadership retreat. This intense time allowed my students to immerse themselves in the world of leadership and establish the lines of communication and bonds of friendship that would allow us to not only survive, but thrive for the upcoming year. I tried to be creative about finding ways to offset the costs for the students, including using a booster subsidy and cabins that belonged to parents so that everyone could participate at little to no cost. During these forays into the forest, each section was assigned a meal to prepare for the entire leadership team, which shared our responsibilities and provided for great fun. The kids would fight over the meal they wanted to cook (breakfast, lunch or dinner) so they could prepare their signature dish, which would inevitably outdo what had been prepared the year before. On two occasions during my fifteen years on the podium, we were unable to travel due to fire and water restrictions, so I hosted the event at my house. The effect was still the same as we were able to tune out the outside world and tune into each other. I am convinced that these retreats were the foundation of our success each year as they

TRAVEL TIP

If you can't get the group away for three days, which I highly recommend, then do a one-night sleepover at someone's house.

allowed for a frank and honest dialogue and in-depth planning time that would not be available in any other format. Each year the schedule, curricula and activities at these retreats would change slightly to meet the needs of the band and learning styles of the team. There were always an abundant amount of games, which would provide humor and learning at the same time.

One time, I loaded the kids into the van, dropped them off in the middle of a nearby small town and asked them to go on a scavenger hunt. They were each given a list of things to find and were required to show tangible proof of each item. The list included LOVE, HONOR, DIGNITY, RESPECT, LOYALTY, COMMITMENT, and CARING. They were given one hour to work in groups and were told to meet at a nearby ice cream stand with their results, where we shared laughter, joy and some tears over single-scoop ice cream cones. It was truly touching to hear the stories of the people they met and what they had learned during their one-hour adventure. Kids came back with notes from couples who had been married for forty years, fur from a passing puppy dog, a family picture from a local townsperson and so much more. Most importantly, they brought back an appreciation for the qualities I was seeking to instill in them and real-life proof that those qualities existed in the "outside" world.

As each year passed, my personal knowledge regarding leadership training increased. This allowed me to add new material, change old material and invent new games and activities to get my point across to my students. Even though many students attended the weekend workshop in successive years, the experience was never the same. In addition to all of the changes, I was able to narrow the focus of our time together to the things I felt were the most important and would yield the greatest results for the organization.

After fifteen years, I narrowed the curricula to six areas that I feel best prepared the students for success in my group. They are as follows:

Purpose - What is the purpose of our group? What is the purpose of the leadership team?

Performance - How have you performed as a leader in the past year? How can you improve?

Parameters - What should the leadership team do and what should they not do?

Picture - What is the "BIG PICTURE?" Are you looking at things from all angles?

Process - How do we do what we do? Who should be doing what?

Presence - Are we a force in our group, both in the planning and execution process?

This is not to say that there are not other worthy areas of discussion. Certainly there are. It has been my experience, though, that most necessary conversations can be had through one or more of these areas and that when put together, they will give you a foundation upon which to build your individualized leadership program. If care is taken to ensure that everyone sees the bigger picture and has the correct point of focus, the smaller issues can be dealt with by the students themselves.

As you can tell, I am an advocate of experiential learning. I think people learn more when they participate in the process. Beyond the experience, it creates a greater sense of "buying" into the product as well as the process. This means that you will only get out of this what you put into it. The more you choose to be involved in the creation process, the more influence and input you will have in the type of group you are and the quality of year you are about to experience. The following six units will allow you a great deal of insight and input into how your group operates and what direction it is headed in. What you make of it is up to you – remember, traveling in a group is different than traveling alone. All aboard, let's load the train!

SCOTT LANG'S LEADERSHIP TRAVEL GUIDE

 # SCAVENGER HUNT

Have a scavenger hunt within your school, community, or organization. Make a list of things you are looking for which are the most meaningful for you. Group the students into appropriately and even-sized teams and send them off with a check sheet and instructions that they must come back with some sort of physical evidence. You may even want to make it a video scavenger hunt using cameras or cell phones with camera capabilities.

166

Purpose: Why Take the Trip at All?

Every trip has a purpose. Some trips are for pleasure, some for fun, some are personal and some are professional. Many trips are usually a mixture of all of the above. It does not matter why you travel, just so long as everyone understands and agrees about the end result that you are seeking. On a trip, when one person packs all of their business suits and another packs nothing but bathing suits, you are in trouble. So, what is the purpose of your leadership trip and what are you packing: things for fun, things for work, or a mixture of both? Did anyone think to include a first aid kit?

Most students believe that there is a single-minded purpose for their group and that it is obvious for one and all to see. They believe this because, like many of us, they assume that everyone thinks like they do. We often assume that our perspectives are everyone's perspectives. This is not necessarily out of selfishness but due to the fact that everyone lives in their own world 24/7, with a somewhat egocentric (but human) point of view. If you were to press these students with a question about the purpose of band, they would probably give you their answers and assume that all other students agree with them, when in fact, there are a variety of reasons for band that meet a variety of student needs. They rarely mention that the study of music provides a well-rounded education and has been demonstrated to assist learning and brain function in other curricular areas, which is what a lot of teachers might say.

Let's start with one possible reason that meets one of the most basic of needs. Everybody wants to be accepted. Abram Maslow demonstrated in his now-famous Hierarchy of Needs that every person wants to be a part of a group. In fact, that is one of the primary reasons gangs exist, as they allow people with no other formal group structure somewhere to "belong." Is the need to belong to something greater than yourself an important one? Just ask the gang members who are willing to die for it. The lengths people will go to be a part of something is startling at times. High school campuses are maybe the greatest social model of this theory we know of. Students will dress a certain way, talk a certain way, act a certain way and even engage in behaviors that are unhealthy and contrary to their belief systems all in the name of acceptance. All in all, the desire for belonging can be a powerful one.

In regards to school music programs specifically, here is a list of some of the many other reasons someone may choose to be a part of your group:

> *Some join your group for the strictly for the social aspects.*
> *Some join your group strictly for the musical fulfillment.*
> *A very few join your group because they are required to.*
> *Some join your group because they enjoy the group dynamic.*
> *Some join your group for the love of performing.*

It has been my experience that a vast majority of students join groups due in some part to a combination of the answers given above. Most students would be hard-pressed to single out just one reason that would exclude all others. However, there are those in your midst who have a single-minded sense of purpose when it comes to your program, and those students tend to be very successful in the pursuit of their objective, be it popularity or performance. The question remains, how do you build a program or ensemble that meets the needs of both types of students?

MAKE A MAP

Make a huge map for your classroom, showing not only your starting point and destinations (your goals) for the year, but some of the sights you will see along the way. You may want to include "alternate paths" that could be choices that your group helps to decide. The map could cover an entire classroom wall. This can be as big or as small of a project as your group would like to make it. Be sure to include a packing list appropriate to your destination.

PICTURE MOMENT

Did you join your group for a single-minded purpose or was it for a variety of reasons?

What were they?

The first question you have to ask yourself is: ***"What are we trying to achieve and who are we trying to serve?"*** I know that you may be wondering what, if anything, this has to do with being a student leader. The answer is A LOT. I look at this information as something of a road map to success. If you feel comfortable working your way around this question, then you may not need to refer to it, but keep in mind that you are responsible for people who may not know where they are going and you have to help get them there. You do not need to look at the map described previously (or discuss it) every time you get ready to depart on your journey, but the one answer that you need it for may prove to be the one that keeps you from wasting a great deal of time, effort and frustration. This kind of map doesn't require any tricks to fold it back up, either.

Like it or not, the law of the land guarantees fair and equal education for all students. Believe it or not, this means that teachers **must** meet the needs of all students, even when those needs are in opposition to each other. For instance, how do you build a group for John Smith, who is just taking the class for a Fine Arts credit and still meet the needs of Debbie Jones, who would like to pursue music as a career after high school? One is interested in the serious pursuit of the arts while the other is just looking for an easy A and a way to fill out their schedule. To further complicate matters, they may both be in the same class, but they are in it for very different reasons. This is just one example of many deep and involved questions regarding the validity of your program. That was just a warm-up question…here are some more questions for you to think about or your leadership team to discuss:

Since I was a music teacher, I will use music examples, but most of these can apply to any group.

- How do you afford a jazz experience to all of your students when there are limitations based on talent and quality of instrumentation?

- Is it fair to require more practice time from a flautist that is it is of a percussionist?

- How do you meet the needs of all musicians when your school only has one concert group?

- How do you challenge your best musicians without frustrating your weakest musicians?

- How do you hold high performance standards when students who cannot afford that type of time investment due to family- or work-related circumstances are a part of your program?

- How do we ensure that all students receive an equal education regardless of socio-economic status? Instruments cost money. Reeds cost money. Trips cost money. Private lessons cost money. Honor ensembles cost money. The list goes on and on.

- How do you invest in issues related to character education when it means less rehearsal time for the actual music itself?

- How do you balance innovation and excellence and appropriate balance between band and other life and school responsibilities?

Friction and frustration are often a result of these travel plans not having been thoroughly discussed and explored. In limited cases, where there are very large and evolved music programs with multiple opportunities in the areas of concert, jazz, marching, chamber ensembles and a variety of staff to meet the demand in these areas, this is less of an issue. Students may have a menu of musical opportunities from which to choose and can make an appropriate selection based on their ability to make a personal and musical investment. This may not eliminate the problem, but it may make it less of an issue. However, in most programs, this is not the case and hard choices need to be made based on equity (not equality), the values of the director and the school community.

))TRAVEL ADVISORY

Look up the definitions of equity and equality and talk about which is more important to a student's experience in your program. There may only be a difference of two letters between these words, but their meanings are worlds apart.

These choices are difficult enough to tackle on their own, but they don't take into consideration those related to the development of musical skills versus character development. Though I used the term "versus," I want to make clear that these issues are not in opposition, but rather that both require a portion of our most valued and diminishing asset: TIME. How do we choose between two equally noble destinations? How do we choose to see the Eiffel Tower over the Louvre? How do you choose the Grand Canyon over Mount Rushmore? How do you compare Times Square to Tiananmen Square? There is no win/win here.

CAR GAME

Have a discussion with your group using these questions and ones that you come up with on your own.

Unfortunately, the vast majority of students will not pursue music as a vocation after high school. Does this make their time spent making music more important or less important? Here are some more questions to consider:

Of what value is the three-octave chromatic scale to the soon-to-be economics major?

Of what value is proper embouchure placement to the soldier serving in an armed conflict?

Of what value is music theory to the mother of three trying to make ends meet?

Of what value is music at all?

Certainly, few would argue that developing both character and music skills are worthy pursuits for a school music program. But with increased demands and diminished resources, sometimes decisions have to be made that reflect the individual value systems of the school community and music organization. Even within the same school, the band, orchestra and choir may choose different variations on the same theme or a different theme altogether. The football team may have a different mission than the baseball team. The yearbook may approach journalism differently than the school newspaper. To make the discussion hit a little closer to home (my home):

Should we choose easier music so as to provide students with the opportunity for success?

Should we be creating better music "consumers" instead of performers?

Should we choose easier music and perform concerts more regularly?

Should we provide more chamber ensembles and fewer full ensembles so as to be able to group students by talent and interest?

Should we purchase uniforms, which are incredibly expensive, when most programs are struggling to provide for and maintain their instrument inventory?

Now that I have most likely piqued some curiosities and raised some eyebrows, let's go back to the original question at hand: What is the purpose of your group? Why is it important and who are you trying to serve? Furthermore, TO WHAT END ARE YOU SERVING AND WHY?

What type of student do you invest the most in?
What types of students are you serving the least?
Why do we spend money on non-musical pursuits (color guard, marching staff, materials)?

CAR GAME

How does your program reflect its school community?

Furthermore, how does your program reflect today's changing times?

Does it look and feel as it did twenty years ago? Is that good or bad?

Throughout the bulk of my career, I served in areas that were challenged from a socio-economic standpoint. A great many of my students had never been to a formal concert, been on a plane or had a family member attend college. In a situation such as this, should this information affect my curricula? Should I be offering Mariachi Band instead of orchestra? Should I be offering ethno-music courses instead of music theory? Should this factor into the experiences I needed to provide such as trips or guest clinicians? Should this affect my philosophy of music education by emphasizing more character education? Should I challenge students in this type of socioeconomic situation to rise above their surroundings by challenging them in a way no one else has, or be mindful that these students have greater concerns than my class? By changing the standards based on their personal situation and surroundings, would I be helping or hurting them?

POSTCARD

Who is popular in your group?

Who gets called on the most?

Who is respected?

Who is feared?

Are different ages treated differently?

Are boys and girl treated differently?

What sections or parts of your group are valued more?

What sections or parts of your group are valued less?

What behaviors get attention?

From whom do they get attention?

Is the attention good or bad?

These are important questions with answers that have far-reaching effects. Your teacher may choose to share with you his/her thoughts on these matters and how those thoughts came about or you may just be turned loose to see what happens. There are no right or wrong answers. There are no simple answers. There are only YOUR answers. These are the answers that you can agree on and take responsibility for. Either way, know that you are making a difference in the life of every student you come into contact with.

Purpose of Tour Guides: Why Have Leaders?

Okay, so your brain is hurting from the enormity of the previous discussion. This may be a chance to regroup and address some more straightforward questions. Then again, this could end up in a street brawl between the guard section leader and the drum line captain. I won't tell you who I would put my money on, but a six-foot pole outreaches a twelve-inch stick any day of the week. Then again, drummers have the distinct advantage of having body armor built into their equipment. Metal poles, body armor…is this marching band or the Middle Ages?

So, you have a leadership team. YEAH! You and your student leader colleagues have been selected as tour guides of this nine-month journey. You are the stewards of the trip. Leaders are there to ensure that everything goes well and that everyone has a good time. Your job is not to see the sights, but to make sure that the sights are there to be seen. Your job is not to entertain, but to see that entertainment is to be had. Your job is to make sure that when all is said and done, everyone in your charge has had a worthwhile and memorable experience.

Why should we have student leaders as tour guides? What is the point of tour guides at all? What is it that you and your student leader peers bring to the table that you could not hire someone to do as effectively and even more efficiently? Honestly, if you look at leadership strictly as a job, you have to wonder from a cost-benefit standpoint what your benefit is versus the costs. The costs of student leaders generally do not come in dollars and cents but in mistakes made and frustration caused. Student leaders can generally accomplish a great deal of good, but when they make mistakes, they tend to make some BIG ones.

Do the benefits for you and your peers outweigh the potential deficit? Can't we just let everyone off the bus and go see what they want to see?

Since saving the money to hire someone to do the jobs you are doing is not really an option, I believe the most significant reason for utilizing student leaders is fostering the growth of young people, leaders and followers alike. Student leaders not only serve to create an environment where they help their peers grow and succeed, but go through the same process simultaneously as a leader. Through student leaders, everyone grows. Does your group have an educational goal for the student leadership team or are you all merely task managers? Do you know what you want to accomplish after having been in this group or are you just along for the ride? Have you ever taken the time to assess your progress in pursuit of your own and your group's leadership goals? YES, ASSESS AND TEST! We test for everything else in school; so how do we test for leadership?

Before we can begin to assess, we have to decide what it is that we are looking for. We have to decide what it is we are trying to accomplish with not only your group, which we covered in the last chapter, but with your student leadership team. The best way to do that is by asking some simple questions:

> *What is the purpose of our leadership team?*
>
> *How is that different from last year?*
>
> *What were our greatest issues of concern last year with our group?*
>
> *What changes have we made to this year's council to address those issues?*
>
> *Does having a student in charge of some tasks compromise both the efficiency and the quality of our team?*
>
> *Is our team mostly used for one particular class and ignored in others? If so, why?*

Is the team as important in the spring as they are in the fall? If not, why?

Should student leaders be given the opportunity to fail so as to experience personal growth, even if other students pay the price?

I saved the most difficult questions for last:

If the experience of being a student leader is so valuable and important, why do we not rotate the positions every so often so as to give everyone this growth opportunity?

If the goal of student leadership is to enhance educational experience, then which comes first, great groups or great student leadership?

Finally, if a tree falls in the woods and no one is around to hear it, can we chop it up and use the paper to print this book?

CAR GAME

Have a frank and honest discussion with your team after everyone has reviewed the questions. Be sure to allow your director the first and last opportunity to speak to each issue as he/she is the decision maker.

Most student leaders will not be able to fully answer all of questions listed above. There are a great many issues involved and you may not have enough information or training in these areas to fully answer the questions. This is an excellent time to listen to your director explain his/her belief system about student leadership and ask questions.

Your input is important here, but not as important as your understanding. Your teacher has built a belief system based on his/her professional experience and advanced training. This is not the time for you to redefine leadership as you see it, but find a place in the system where you can fill a need within the framework your teacher creates.

You may be the professional tour guide, but that does not mean you can tell the pilot how to fly the plane. You both have a critical role, but you have to know when to step up and when to step aside. For the purposes of this part of the discussion, the pilot is in charge.

I hate to use a bad cliché, but I will: we all work for someone. We may not always understand why they do things the way they do or how they have arrived at their belief system, but there always comes a time when we question their instructions. If you don't agree with the boss, even if you feel that your point of disagreement is valid, should you still obey? Now I'm going to quote your parents: "You should do it because I said so." This is certainly not the most educational response, but it is more efficient and effective when it comes to dealing with some issues. You would not want someone to question everything you do in front of your peers, so make sure not to do the same to your teacher in front of other students. Simply put, you work for your teacher. You may not get paid, but you applied for the job, so you can't say that it is forced labor. Now it is time to hear what your boss has to say. As with any boss, it would be a good idea to listen with an open heart and mind to what he/she has to say, not only because it is the right thing to do, but because your director may have some important information to share.

We are living in a culture that questions everything. Given today's media and the accessibility of information, we are living in a world of shrinking boundaries. There is no subject we feel is taboo and no end to what we believe we have the "right" to know about our leaders and those we work for. Our leaders have been held to a higher standard and greater scrutiny than any other time in history. You can do an Internet search and find out what the CEO of a company makes, drives, and eats for dinner. Useful information? Probably not, but there it is anyway. This is true because when you are at the CEO level of leadership, you leave the "real" world behind.

Anyone who differs with me on this would have to explain how making thirty million dollars through stock options when the company is bankrupt is living in the real world.

In the end, you applied for a job as a student leader. It should be abundantly clear whom you work for. The roles and responsibilities should be well-defined and as clear as possible for all to see. This will help everyone involved keep from getting confused about where the boundaries are. Understand that if you are going to question the philosophies and decisions of your teacher, you would be well-suited to do so in private where your concerns can be addressed in a more individual manner, or polish up your résumé. So let me be clear – now is the time to listen as your boss explains what the purpose of student leaders are and what he/she expects you to do!

Good luck and good listening!

POSTCARD

As a team, create a list of five things a leader in your group should always do without being asked. Then create a list of five things that a leader in your group should never do. Finally, create a list of five things you wish would be done to help make the group better. This will help to set up a framework of boundaries. Post these rules on a leadership bulletin board and review them every once in awhile at leadership meetings.

Performance: Their Joy is Your Job

Performance, when placed in the context of music, is usually thought of as being limited to the stage, recital hall or football field. At the very least, the term elicits thoughts of an audience of some sort. This, however, is not the definition of performance that we are after. More specifically, we are going to discuss job performance. As student leaders, you will be judged both individually and collectively on your ability to meet the prescribed needs of your job.

First of all, from a musical performance viewpoint, the requisites for success are pretty concrete and have been embedded in us since we first picked up our instruments. Successful qualities may include musical responsibilities like playing correct notes and rhythms, playing within the framework of the group and utilizing proper pitch and tone. Finally, they may also include visual responsibilities such as adherence to uniform codes, correct marching technique, bow angles, posture, choreography, intervallic control, step size, hand position, horn angles, etc…. Whatever your standard of measurement, there are some fairly clear indicators of success and failure for the ensemble members to measure themselves against. Furthermore, most students have a very clear understanding of what is expected and how to determine whether or not they are meeting with success.

CAR GAME

What if we had a festival for leaders where respected and experienced people in the field of leadership adjudicated your performance? You could explain to them your job performance and they could provide feedback on how to be a better leader. Would that be beneficial? If so, why not do it with your own group?

As for group performance, we have created an especially torturous process from which to elicit feedback called festivals. This is when we pay professionally trained adjudicators to fire cannonballs of criticism at us while we stand on stage. You might as well place a huge target on the director's back.   For an extra special added treat (as if the performance in a strange hall after a two-hour bus ride was not enough), we get to sight-read for the first time in front of someone who has heard the piece of music at least thirty times while he/she makes observations of the obvious – like "watch out for the key change" (as if we could do something about it at that point). Telling a group that just sight-read a piece to "watch out for the key change" is like telling someone to "watch out for the bus" after their funeral. Believe it or not, as painful as they are, these events are designed to give us feedback and assist us in personal and professional growth. They are educational in nature and give the ensemble an opportunity to meet with people who are experienced and are generally respected in their field. We do this all in the name of educational growth.

If this process is so important, why do we not do something similar with leadership? Why don't we evaluate you as a leader the way we evaluate you as a player? Think about it – it makes some sense. The fact is, we do not spend as much, if any, time evaluating ourselves as leaders, but if we want to improve our leadership skills, it is important to spend some time assessing what we have done and how we have done it. Consider the questions below your performance assessment. Before answering, be sure to paint a big target on your back and strap on your thin skin! Remember, be as honest and unbiased as possible.

 POSTCARD

Were you successful last year in the area of leadership performance?

Were you more successful in rehearsal or in performances as a leader?

Was there an individual who was influenced in any way by your performance?

If so, who? How was he/she influenced?

Was it positive or negative?

Did you perform up to your capabilities?

If not, where did you falter?

Performance evaluation, when placed in the context of leadership, should not be all that dissimilar from music. And yet, it often is. I believe that we should be able to assess a leader's performance in given tasks so as to be able to measure growth and progress. Granted, it will not always be as obvious or easy, say, as checking for right notes or correct horn angles, but is equally as important for your individual growth and the growth of the ensemble. The old adage of "when the water rises, so do all things that float" applies here. In this case, as the quality of the leaders rise, so do all things in the group. **The better we train our leaders, the better we train our group!**

Like music, leadership requires you to meet certain performance standards. The standards may be subjective and differ from group to group, but there are standards nonetheless. If someone were unwilling to meet the responsibilities associated with being a member of the ensemble, they would most likely be removed. At the very least, that person's role would be diminished so as to reflect their level of commitment. Your role as a leader is no different. It has responsibilities that you are required to perform. These responsibilities are different and are in addition to your requisite duties as a member of the ensemble. Should you fail to meet them, your performance review should reflect that and your leadership role should be diminished. You would not give the solo in the show to someone who never showed up to practice, so why would you give responsibility to someone who fails to "show up" as a leader?

There is an old saying that states, "If you want something done, ask a busy person." Have you ever noticed that your director continually relies on a small group of people to get things done? Some people call these students "teacher's pets" or "favorites." This is somewhat ironic, given the fact that by being a "pet" or a "favorite," these people are asked to do more work. When you think about it that way, the word favor really is an appropriate root word for favorite. Do you really want to be the favorite?

PICTURE MOMENT

What does your teacher ask of you?
If the answer is very little, you may want
to ask if there is a reason for that. You
might find out that you have been getting
exactly what he/she thought you could
handle...very little! Let your director know
if and when you are ready for more. As,
you know by now, the more you give, the
more you get. However, the more you get,
the more you have to give!

How do we define and assess the performance of a leader? Well, a good place to start is the job description for your position. What, you say that there is none?

Well then, it is time to write one.

JOB POSTING

On a different sheet of paper, please write a "Job Posting" for your position. If your position is filled by multiple students, then you may work as a group to come up with your ad. I encourage you to think your job through completely before writing the ad. For instance, you may at first describe your leadership position in very generic terms, like "chef." How would we know what this job entails? I would bet that a job posting for a pastry chef in a five-star resort would look different than that of a line cook in the Marines, embedded in the frontline of a combat situation. To that same end, I think the job of percussion section leader is VERY different than that of color guard captain or drum major. Spend some time REALLY thinking about your job and what it requires of you every day to do it successfully.

Some things you may want to consider before writing are:

Is personal character an issue?

Can anyone apply?

Are there age restrictions on the applicants (can incoming freshmen apply)?

Is experience required? If so, what: leadership, musicianship or both?

What training will be provided? Is it provided before or after selection?

Do the job hours extend outside of school? If so, by how much?

Would you expect an applicant to be a leader in English class as well? How would you know?

Is grade point average a factor?

Will you require reference checks?

What should every applicant know before applying?

JOB POSTING cont'd

In your posting you should consider including the following items:

List of responsibilities: discipline, running sectionals, music checks, car washes, meetings, etc...

Description of duties (be as specific as possible)

Time commitments and hours

List of benefits

A complete list of requisite skills (playing and otherwise)

Length and term of service

Limitations on applicants, physical and otherwise

When you are done, give your ad a catchy title and post it for everyone to see or read it to the group. See what the commonalities and differences are about the positions. After hearing everyone else's descriptions, is there anything you would add to your job description? Is there anything you missed? Did anything anyone else said change your views on leadership?

It's more than likely that this task was a little harder than you had originally thought. That is not your fault. Oftentimes, we create positions and select student leaders but never really explore what the job involves and what we really expect from them. In this scenario, our leaders have no alternative but to repeat what was done "to them" and "for them" by previous student leaders. Is this really the best way to get the most out of your leadership team?

Now it is time for the most important question of all.

Now that you have a true understanding of what is expected, are you still convinced that you are, in every way, the right person for this job? How do your strengths align with the job requirements and where might you need assistance in order to meet the needs of the position? If you are feeling like you may fall short in some areas, don't worry; someone is there to help. There are also elements of your job that you are very good at that others may need your help with to be successful. There are elements of every job that suit our strengths and elements of every position that expose our weaknesses. This is part of the personal growth process. If you are willing to both give and accept help from others, you will grow as a person and the group will grow as an ensemble. Remember the saying about "as the water rises…"

Remember, you applied for this job. You had a pretty good idea that as a tour guide you would have less fun and more work than those under your supervision. You knew that their happiness was your job. You knew you would need to be the first one on the bus and the last one off. You knew all of this when you signed on to be their tour guide. You made the decision to pursue this position. There is no acceptable excuse for not doing it to the very best of your abilities.

CAR GAME

Now would be a good time to go around the room and share your greatest strength as it relates to the position and your greatest area of concern. This will allow you to hear those who have strengths in your area of need and vice versa. Speak up, be heard and help a friend.

Parameters of the Trip: Acting as One

Every job has parameters, even leadership. In order for the many to act as one, and for all tasks to go smoothly, there must be a clear understanding about what you can and cannot do as a part of your leadership role and job as a tour guide. This is for your comfort as well as that of the group. Many people say they do not like to play by the rules, but in the end, most creatures – animal and human alike – find comfort in operating within given parameters. Leaders are no different in this way; we find comfort in knowing what we can and can't do. These boundaries help to keep us safe and allow us to feel successful within a protective environment. These confines are there for your benefit, so learn to understand, appreciate and embrace them.

The parameters under which you work will vary from person to person, group to group, year to year, and may even vary from position to position. If you choose to be a leader who merely repeats the behaviors of others, than you should have remained a follower. Flexibility in altering these rules is not only allowed but is encouraged. Some of the parameters may focus on experience. Some may be focused on your training and experience (or lack thereof). Other boundaries may be more arbitrary and deal more with the comfort level of the teacher(s) making the decisions. Whatever the reason, you need to be willing to accept that in most cases, leaders are selected with equity (the best fit for you) and not equality (the same fit for everyone) in mind.

You just finished the exercise Job Posting, which basically describes what your job **IS**.

Now the question needs to be asked: What is your job **NOT**?

The job description you created can serve as an excellent beginning point for establishing parameters. In fact, now would be a good time to pull it back out and review it. If you have not already done so, ask your director and your fellow student leaders to share theirs by reading them out loud. Make notes as to any differences between your perceived boundaries and others, most importantly your director's. Where are there overlaps and similarities and where are there stark differences?

There are a thousand things that you may be asked NOT to do in your role as a leader, but I have found that most mature students can figure these out for themselves (we have to explain them to the drummers). If you could not operate at this level of decision-making, you would not be considered a leader. In fact, I doubt that they will ever take as much responsibility as I am willing to give. After all, what teacher would not want to have a group full of people taking too much responsibility? *In all of my years of teaching and training, I have only had two students evolve their leadership role into its fullest possible scenario and they were the two best student leaders I have ever worked with.* You are a creative, intelligent and ethical human being or you would not be a leader. You know right from wrong, when you do it and when you see it. Now, do you have the courage to correct it?

I could go on and on about the specific behaviors that are acceptable as a student leader, but I would be assuming that everyone viewed leadership the same way I do. However, there are four areas which experience tells me are the most troubling to student leaders and directors alike. The following questions are designed to start the discussion process.

- *Do the responsibilities of my position extend outside of the rehearsal hall? (If someone from band is acting inappropriately in gym class, am I to say something?)*

- *How far outside of the class or campus is my purview of responsibility? (If someone is acting up in church, am I to respond?) Where are the boundaries?*

- *If a staff member is present, should I respond to issues or assume that the staff member or director will address them as they see fit? In a rehearsal setting, when should I serve as a leader and when should I serve as a follower?*

- *Do I have the conscience to know right from wrong and the courage to stand for it on a consistent and continual basis?*

TRAVEL TIP

After you have completed these discussions, make sure everyone adds any new elements to their job description. This will ensure that everyone is on the same page!

There are no clear-cut answers to these questions. Each director and each program has their own way of responding to behavioral issues. Some teachers see students as students no matter where they are and when it is, while others view their responsibility in a more restricted way. How does your teacher view it? Is it different from the way you view it? If so, how will you reconcile your differences? As teachers, we would all like to hold our students to the highest standards in all situations, in and out of the rehearsal hall, but how realistic is this? How important is this? How do we go about achieving this?

To provide a more detailed discussion, here are some more specific points to consider...

- *Am I allowed to discipline the members I am in charge of?*

- *What is an appropriate way to discipline?*

- *What issues should be addressed by a student leader, and what issues should be left to the staff?*

- *What does district or school policy prohibit you from doing (handling keys, taking attendance, using the copier, etc...)?*

- *What does band policy prohibit me from doing (addressing things while director is talking, yelling, assigning grades, etc...)?*

- *When am I a leader, and when do I need to be more subservient?*

- *What are my director's pet peeves?*

- *Does something I do fit into that category? Do I need to change?*

- *Should we deal only with the members in our charge or can a guard captain deal with a member of the drum line?*

- *Is there a hierarchy within the band council in terms of chain of command?*

- *Is there anyone in your charge that you feel uncomfortable leading? If so, what are the issues relating to this situation?*

Being an effective leader is like dealing with the Internal Revenue Service. You may do everything right for a significant period of time and hear nothing from the federal government, but when you do something wrong, they will be camped out on your doorstep ready to pounce. For the sake of this analogy, consider your teacher the IRS. Pay equal attention to what you should NOT do as well as what you SHOULD do, otherwise you are likely to be the subject of a leadership audit...OUCH!

I mentioned several times earlier in this book that I do not think there are any golden rules to leadership. I can no more create a list of things to do than I can of things not to do. In the end, you have to be comfortable with your relationship with the teacher and with your role as a leader. Everything after that is just using your judgment and behaving in a manner that demonstrates integrity, respect and the values of your individual program. With those three things, you can create your own checklist to follow. Send it to me; I could use one.

Pictures: Big and Small

Earlier in the book, I spoke about my love for pictures. I do LOVE pictures. I love the memories they represent and history they save. Pictures are my way of compensating for my extremely poor memory. Trust me when I say that this is not an act of vanity, as I am not someone who is particularly photogenic. I try too hard to look good in pictures, which inevitably makes me look bad in pictures, which makes me try harder to look better in pictures, etc. It is an ugly, vicious cycle.

The problem with pictures is that they are just a small representation of an actual experience, a sliver of time that represents a much greater cycle of events. Beyond that, they are not often an accurate reflection of what really happened. Sure,

PICTURE MOMENT

What is your favorite picture and why? What does it show and how is that different from what it represents?

they document the little things – height, hair color, the type of clothes you wear – but not necessarily do they capture the feelings and emotions of a moment. Have you ever smiled for a photo when you were having a lousy time? Does that Thanksgiving photo represent how you were really feeling after dinner – bloated, overstuffed and hopped up on tryptophan to the point of being borderline comatose? NO! We all smile for the camera and pretend that all is well because that is the BIG picture we want to preserve; a day spent in the company of those we love.

CAR GAME

Is there a single picture of your group that fairly represents it?

Maybe it is after winning a competition or celebrating a successful performance. Does it accurately reflect the two-hour bus ride, the uncomfortable uniforms, the hot stage lights? What would the perfect picture of your group look like?

This would be a great show and tell activity for your group.

Unlike a camera, your memory can capture infinite amounts of both small- and big- picture moments and construct them into a memory that will last a lifetime. Let's just say that your mind has one SERIOUSLY large memory card. It knows what finite elements are relevant and how they fit into the larger picture of life. The ability to filter through mass amounts of information and stimuli and piece specific fragments together into a single thought or memory is an impressive feat that confounds even the world's greatest supercomputer, and yet you do it every day. In fact, you are doing it right now. Your mind is in constant motion: gathering information, sorting, storing, processing and collating little bits of it into a single, significant "picture" for you to reflect upon. We do it every moment of every day; why not do it with our groups?

We have all heard the expression "can't see the forest for the trees." It is an old saying that extols the virtue of seeing the larger picture as opposed to what is immediately obvious. We frequently get too caught up in our daily activities, failing to stay focused on the larger and sometimes more important picture. Take your high school, for instance. When was the last time you as a student thought about scheduling, facilities management, staffing, bond expenditures, textbook selection, school funding, security, athletics, and educational philosophy as it related to your education? What, you say you have spent the last ten years or so immersed in this educational institution, eight hours a day or more, and never given this any thought? Are you trying to tell me you have no idea how often the oil on the bus is changed, the tires are rotated, or who orders and delivers the thousands of items you hungry students consume every day? Of course not; you were too busy thinking about homework, or lunch, or what you were going to do later on that evening. Just getting through the day to sixth period is about all most of you think about…well, all that you could print in this book, anyway.

PICTURE MOMENT

For just one day, take a look around your school and see how many people other than teachers make it run; bus drivers, cafeteria workers, groundskeepers, referees, library aides, etc… You might begin to appreciate your school for the small city that it is.

To be an effective leadership travel guide, you have to be able to think about where your group will be in ten days as well as where the group will be in ten minutes. There is no detail too small to escape your attention, but more importantly, no issue too big for your input. For instance, in my first trip as a teacher, while on a trip to a city I had never visited, my group was caught in the middle of a city-wide riot, which cut off our access to our hotel, the festival and most of our attractions. Pre-planned meals and attractions were missed and events were canceled. We were forced to schedule pizza parties and poolside games of charades at the hotel to fill the time. For four days, I kept one eye on the kids, who were within my domain of control, and one eye on the television, adjusting to things that were out of my control. This was my baptism by fire as a tour guide.

Why is it important for you to master all of this information, large and small? It will not help you win any trivia contest, nor will any of it come in handy as a time-filler on your next date…unless you are dating a plant. Nor is the purpose of this activity to make you a junior version of your teacher (I am sure we can all agree that one of those is enough). Through this discovery process you will grow to understand the bigger picture of how your large and complex organization operates. This will not only allow you to be more knowledgeable about the program you lead, but will help you to understand how the decision-making process operates and why the program functions the way it does. The next time you hear a student say, "This is stupid," or, "I don't know why we have to do this," you will be able to provide an informed answer.

POSTCARD

Make a list of all of the people who help to make a Friday performance happen. Be sure to include announcers, timekeepers, parent helpers, staff, grounds crew and everyone else who has a part in your success. If it doesn't amaze you, it will humble you – or both.

FINDING PURPOSE

Take a step back, abandon your preconceived notions and evaluate your individual program from a larger perspective. Assess the program comprehensively and answer the questions below. You don't have to write an essay. Just be prepared to discuss your answers with the rest of your leadership team or your sponsor. You might want to jot down some notes on the backside of this page. Share your thoughts with others and see how they compare. You might be surprised!

- What is the purpose of your program?

- Are you performance-driven or education-driven?

- Is the focus of your program where it should be?

- Is there a stated philosophy to the program?

- Does everybody understand the philosophy of the program?

- Is there merit in what you do?

- Should your organization be considered extra-curricular, co-curricular, or curricular? Do you even know the difference?

- What have you really learned as a result of being involved?

- What should you have learned as a result of being involved?

- What is the role of winter guard/guard in this program?

As you answered the questions from the activity, did you think about the impact of your answers on all elements of your music program?

Concert Group 1
Concert Group 2
Concert Group 3
Jazz Band 1
Jazz Band 2
Symphony Orchestra
Marching Band
Winter Guard
Chamber Ensembles

Did you also consider the ramifications of your answers on the following people as a part of your program?

Director
Boosters
Booster officers
Non-booster parents
Students
Staff
Student leaders
Drum major
Elementary/junior high music teachers
Administration
District office

Now for the two big questions – in this world of increasing demands and diminishing time and resources…

1. How does the hierarchy work with the various programs and personnel?

2. Do you allocate time and money in accordance with that hierarchy?

If you and your director can clearly answer the two previous questions, your group is poised for success in whatever it does. If not, there may be some room for improvement. My guess is that you are starting to see that your music program is much more than a class; it is a vibrant and complex organization that requires the work of many people to be successful. Does that change the way you view what you do?

It is not important that you understand the historical reasoning or philosophy behind each and every decision. That would be a waste of your time and your director's. It is important, however, that you see the forest of your program versus just seeing the single tree of your particular class. It is important to know how the effect of the fall color guard affects not only the winter guard, but the concert band as well. It is important to understand the financial impact of having technical staff for some members of the group (percussion and guard) while not providing the same instructional benefits to others. It is important to know why we spend resources on jazz ensembles when they only affect a small amount of students who are usually already receiving musical instruction in another ensemble. You may not participate in any of the above ensembles, but you are a leader and to some extent you are accountable for the decisions that are made about them, or at least understanding and supporting them. Remember, in addition to being your program director, your teacher is also a faculty member of the entire school and has to be able to think and make decisions with a more global understanding of education, no matter what subject he/she teaches.

TRAVEL ADVISORY

Your job as a leader is similar in that the responsibility of knowledge exists beyond your classroom doors.

Think back to the perfect picture I spoke about at the beginning of this chapter. Did it include everyone associated with your program? Did it reflect the performance or the rehearsal process? Did it reflect good and bad times? If you were to take the perfect picture again, would it look any different after having thought about the entire forest?

CAR GAME

This is a great time to ask your tour guide (teacher) any question you want. Don't let your director off the hook; pepper him or her with questions about philosophy, budget, equipment, facilities, festivals, staffing, etc. This is not a time to challenge, just question. Use this process as an opportunity to learn something new. Each and every program is different. Even within the same program, each and every year is different. Music groups are highly dynamic and evolving organizations both artistically and organizationally. Try to understand what it is that you are supposed to be leading and have been or will be involved in for a large part of your life.

Process: Making Your Travel Life Better

People who travel frequently understand that process and protocol are key components to any successful trip. They know how to navigate traffic to the airport and navigate through crowds while at the airport. They even know where the airport's electrical outlets are so they can power up all of their components before taking off. An experienced traveler understands how the plane is boarded, where the best seats are and how to cram fourteen days' worth of clothing into a carry-on bag. They know this because understanding the process and protocol of travel makes them more efficient and effective, not to mention happier. Your role as a leader is no different.

PICTURE MOMENT

Think about it: When driving, the only thing that separates you from a certain and painful death is about five cents' worth of yellow paint and a red light bulb hung up high...well, that and the understanding that everyone who drives a car agrees to follow the same protocol.

Everything in life has a process: the way we shower, the way we sit at assemblies, the way we pay our taxes, the way we drive – all of it says something about who we are and how we organize our day. In the end, that is all a process is – a way to organize the things that make up our day and the way we run our lives. Some of these processes are based on well-researched and well-grounded philosophies on performance and perspective while others are just plain old personal preferences and past experiences.

Few organizations are as obsessive about process as your music group. Think about it – as far as groups go, music groups are TYPE-A groups that border on obsessive-compulsive. You have section leaders, drum majors, officers, squad leaders, assistant directors, staff, equipment managers, concertmasters, librarians, etc…the list goes on and on. If you were to look at a typical Friday night marching band event or a concert festival and count the number of things you do that have a specific and repeated process, you would be astounded. How you take roll, how you warm up, how you load the bus, how you hand out uniforms, how you load the truck, how and where you sit, are just a few of MANY examples of how heavily the music activity is invested in process and procedure.

pro • to • col (noun): 1. the rules of correct or appropriate behavior for a particular group of people or in a particular situation

As for protocol, well, your group is crammed with it. Take the Friday night marching band performance we just talked about – what is appropriate behavior for a marching band during a high school football game? When does the band perform – during halftime or pre-game? Depends on who's the home team and who's the away team. How about stand tunes – when are those appropriate? Not while the football team is running a play, that's for sure.

In order to ensure that these various processes and protocols run smoothly, we utilize a great many student leaders and some adults, each one having a specific task or area of responsibility. **Everyone doing their small part WELL allows the greater organization to function as a whole.** Oftentimes the job requirements of these positions are well-thought-out and developed in such a way as to serve the needs of the group.

The band librarian may have a very clear understanding of how to do her job, but may not understand how it affects the uniform person. The uniform person may be keenly aware of his specific responsibilities with the uniforms but is unaware how that affects how the guard functions. Typically, with each job comes a list of expectations and requisite duties, but where these lists of requirements often fall short is how the various positions interact with each other and the band as a whole.

⦿ TRAVEL TIP

As an activity listed earlier in the book, you should have created a job description. Now would be a good time to go back and amend it to include how you interact with other members of the leadership team and the organization as a whole.

For instance, how do the uniform manager and the equipment manager interact? In what situations does the drum major take control over the band president, or vice versa? Where does purview of student leadership end and that of staff begin? If there is a discipline situation, at what point does a squad leader, section leader, drum major or staff member intercede? These are very complex situations that often have not been explored during the training process.

If you are not sure whether everyone understands what their role is and how they fit within the grand scheme of your group, answer the following questions both individually and as a group:

- *Do you have a clear-cut and systematic "process" and hierarchy for dealing with issues?*

- *Was there ever a time last year when the teacher was not present and there was confusion among the group as to how to handle a specific situation? If so, elaborate and discuss.*

- *Has there ever been a time when a parent member overstepped their bounds?*

- *Has there ever been a time when a staff member overstepped their bounds?*

- *When someone oversteps their boundaries or underperforms, do you think this is due to or confusion about their role or is it just poor judgment on their part?*

- *Is everyone in agreement as to the chain of command?*

- *How are problems addressed and handled within the group? (This might be a good time to go to the back of the book and use a couple of the discussion starters as "what if" questions.)*

I am not suggesting that you spend a great deal of time arguing over who is more important than whom. I am suggesting, however, that a trumpet section leader know what their role is when a member of the flute section is acting inappropriately. I am suggesting that in the absence of the teacher, everyone should be very comfortable with how things should and will function in orchestra class. There is no way that you can prepare for all eventualities, but you can prepare for the most obvious ones. I used to tell my students to prepare for the earthquakes. If you live in an area where there is a high likelihood of an earthquake, you can do one of two things: prepare for one and live or ignore it and die. You cannot plan your entire life around being near an earthquake refuge shelter, but you can make an effort to ensure that you understand the basic survival rules when it comes to this natural disaster. The same can be said for process and protocol in a music group. **You can't prepare for every eventuality that may come your way during the year, but you can plan a basic response to situations that might threaten your leadership team and your group.**

CREATE A FLOW CHART

This would be a good time to do a command flow chart for the leadership team. These charts help to create and define clearly understood chains of command and levels of responsibilities. Even with the 25th Amendment, after President Ronald Reagan was shot, there was a crisis in command and no one was in control of the United States Government.

If you have one in place and you think everyone understands it, have them draw it out as a flow chart and compare the results; you might be surprised.

Draw your flow chart below and discuss it with others until you as a group can agree on one chain of command.

Remember, it is not enough to create a plan; you must educate everyone involved with your program and you must be willing to act. Isn't that the lesson we learned from Hurricane Katrina? The best-laid plans…

CAR GAME

List five things that are likely to go wrong during the year.

Some examples might be:

Your director is sick and has to miss a competition.
A new member, who is aggressive, is disrespectful to his smaller section leader.
You hear of a member who is about to do something he should not do on a trip.
You find out that someone in your group is breaking into lockers and taking things.
You hear someone telling vicious lies about your teacher as revenge for a bad grade.

1.

2.

3.

4.

5.

How would you respond to any one of the situations listed above? What would you do? Do you have a plan in place? As I said, the purpose of this activity is for you to create scenarios that are likely to happen in your group and prepare for those. This is how you prepare for a "natural disaster" in your own group.

After all, an earthquake drill would not have been much help to people living on the Gulf Coast during Hurricane Katrina. You can not always control what happens TO your group, but you can control how you RESPOND to it.

This chapter is designed to give you a chance to establish a commonly accepted chain of command and understand how a leadership team deals with controversy. After all, no one needs an Emergency Management Plan when things are going well. It seems like a waste of time if you labor to come up with one and it sits there and collects dust over time, but when and if you need it, you will be glad you have it. With the large number of students in your group and the wide variety of both public and private situations in which you are placed, in my opinion, you are more likely to need this plan than not. I can't give you a flow chart that will explain what to do in the event of a problem because "no such chart exists!", so take this opportunity to create your own!

Presence: Stories from Band Camp and Beyond

The difference between a leadership team and just a bunch of kids who had leadership titles became glaringly apparent to me one sunny summer evening in August at band camp during my first year at my new school. Just as I had done with my previous leadership teams, I had invested heavily during the summer in a leadership training process that included taking the entire team on a three-day leadership retreat in the mountains, after which we met once a week to map out our new plan of attack. As the new band reported for pre-camp, I felt pretty good about where we were at as a team and the direction in which we were headed. How silly was I? I soon learned that I had trained my leaders in what do when a situation occurred but had not factored in whether or not they were a presence in the organization.

I call it the "Charles Smith Effect" (the name has been changed to protect the guilty). In my first year after changing schools, I took my group out of town for our annual band camp experience. After our after-dinner rehearsal and before our evening meeting, Charles decided to don women's undergarments, insert balloons in the appropriate places, put on a wig and make-up and run up and down the hallways of the dormitory screaming, "I AM WOMAN; HEAR ME ROAR!" He continued this activity through several wings of the dorms until I happened to catch sight of him. I promptly stopped him and, controlling my urge to throw him out of the second-story window, made it very clear to him that his actions were unacceptable. I instructed him to return to his room, clean up, change clothes and return to our final meeting where he would apologize to the band for his actions. Seeing the anger in my eyes, he agreed and quickly retreated back to his room.

Immediately, I asked the leadership team to come to the rehearsal room for a meeting. After they arrived, I shared with them my frustration over what had just happened. As I was nearing the end of my rant (and it was a good one), a senior member of the leadership team, who had just missed being selected as drum major by the previous director, blurted, **"I don't know why you are yelling at us; we didn't do anything!"** It was then that I realized I was in for a very long year. I looked directly into that young lady's eyes and said, "That is exactly my point – he ran right by all of you and YOU DIDN'T DO ANYTHING!" As far as I was concerned, Charles should have been my drum major, as he got everyone to go along with whatever he wanted them to despite the fact that he had only been in band for two weeks.

Charles Smith was a freshman who had been diagnosed with Attention Deficit-Hyperactivity Disorder. His mother enrolled him in band because she thought it would be good for him. (It has been my experience that any time a parent puts a kid in my class because they think it will be good for them ensures that it is going to be bad for me.) His inability to fully control his impulse decision-making was a factor in his behavior. They, on the other hand, had no excuses for their actions, medical or otherwise. They just stood and did nothing as Charles did his best imitation of a trans-gender burlesque show.

In an organization as large as your group, it is virtually impossible to keep anything a secret or perform any subversive act anonymously. Oftentimes, student leaders witness acts as they occur or know of them in advance but fail to act on them for fear of alienating their friends.

CAR GAME

Can you think of a time when you had to step up and deal with your peers in corrective manner? How did you handle it? In retrospect, is there anything you would change about it now? If you are in a group, go around and share these stories, not to review the past but to prepare for the future. Write about it below:

Peer pressure, regardless of age, is an incredibly potent agent and is not limited to young people. **In my opinion, dealing with your peers, adult or student, in an adversarial situation is the HARDEST part of being a student leader.** How many people knew in advance of the improprieties of Enron and said nothing? How many people were aware of the improprieties at WorldCom? How many heard the whispers of possible shootings on school campuses but said nothing? How many people had to have known that something was wrong before 9/11 and failed to act? The reasons for inaction are many – peer pressure, fear, lack of confidence, etc. – but the result is the same. I love the following quote when it comes to dealing with action vs. inaction:

When they came for the communists,
I remained silent;
I was not a communist.

When they locked up the social democrats,
I remained silent;
I was not a social democrat.

When they came for the trade unionists,
I did not speak out;
I was not a trade unionist.

When they came for the Jews,
I did not speak out;
I was not a Jew.

When they came for me,
there was no one left to speak out.

attributed to Pastor Martin Niemöller (1892-1984)

PICTURE MOMENT

Think about a time when you could have and should have acted to stop someone from doing something but choose to do nothing. How do you feel about that choice now? Would you handle it differently if you could? How so?

It takes **courage** to stand up for what you believe in. It is uncomfortable, if not downright painful, to separate yourself from your friends by standing up for what you believe. How many times have people around you talked during class and you said nothing? How often do you see inappropriate behavior from a fellow student and look the other way? How many times has someone in your section skipped a rehearsal and you said nothing? How many times have you heard someone disrespect your director and you stood silent? How many times have you heard language that was degrading to someone else and said nothing? **I ask: are you a presence in your section or organization or just someone who has some training and a title?**

CAR GAME

As far as group behavior and respect goes, discuss the following questions within your group and determine if there is an agreement on how much presence the leadership team has in your organization.

Do you consider your leadership team to have a presence in your organization?

If so, what is their role? How are they viewed?

Does everyone outside of the leadership team understand the roles and responsibilities of the student leaders as well?

Do you have the ability and the willingness to step forward and stop something from happening?

Have you in the past? If so, when?

Do you have a particularly troublesome student(s) in your group?

No one likes to be the "bad guy". No one wants to be the one who "narcs" on someone who did something wrong. But in the end, no one respects the person who saw it all and said nothing. **You have to make the decision about whether you would rather have people's respect or their friendship.** My experience has told me that respect is rooted far deeper and in turn lasts longer than mere adulation. You can have both, but there may come a time when you need to choose between the two, and you need to be prepared to make that differentiation.

I often tell young people that there are times they can be friendly without being a friend. Everyone deserves the same level of respect and kindness, but not everyone will be or should be your friend. If there are situations that put you at odds with your friends, they will understand what you are trying to do and how it serves the greater good. If they don't, they may not have been your REAL friends. Are you prepared to make the sacrifices required to be a REAL presence in your group, or are you just for show?

Think of yourself driving down the road one day. The sun is bright, your mood is even brighter and the top is down on your convertible (you wish)! You are cruising along and you see a traffic cop parked along the side of the road with is radar gun pointed directly at you. What is the first thing you do? The answer most people would give is to SLOW DOWN. Why? No one said that you were speeding. For most people, the mere presence of the officer causes you to respond in such a manner that tells you to respond first and ask questions later. Is it out of fear of getting a ticket or of respect for the law and its intent to protect everyone on the roads that you decelerate? Probably a little of both. Like it or not, the officer has a presence and can have an effect on how you behave. Your leadership team should have a similar effect on your group. Should Charles have done the right thing out of respect for the group or out of fear of having to deal with his section leader? The answer? **Probably a little of both.**

If you stand as one, there is no person or persons that can keep you from achieving your goal. You can't possibly expect the band to stand as one and be a presence in your school until the leaders stand as one and serve as a presence for the band.

PICTURE MOMENT

During a Friday night football game some years ago, I saw the confirmation of a band's not only being a presence in the school, but in the community as well. Prior to the game, the band was lining up next to the band room in preparation for the march to the stadium, just as they always had. As the marching block of 160 kids began to make its way to the stadium, a group of "bangers" (slang for gang members), as the kids called them, started to pass through one of the ranks. As I made my way to the young men to keep the rest of them from breaking our ranks, I heard one of them call out to the rest, "Hey, don't walk through the band, man...show some respect; they are BAD A**!" Strange as it sounds, that was the day I knew the band was a presence in that community.

Are your student leaders a presence in your band? Is your band a presence in your community? Stand together, stand strong, but STAND for something!

PACKING LIST

Which of the six elements of leadership were you the least knowledgeable about?

Which of the elements are you best at and worst at? Why?

How were your skills different from your peers? Who in the group can help you and who in the group can you help? Be specific as to how.

Did you learn anything new about your program? If so, what?

After this unit, how are you better prepared to be a leader in your group?

PACKING LIST cont'd

As we near the end of your journey, do you feel more prepared to serve as a guide? How so?

Where are you still not prepared?

How can you become more prepared?

Do you have all of your travel documents (notes/activities from this chapter)? If not, what documents are you lacking (list activities you did not do here, so you can come back another time and work on them)?

✦ TRAVELOGUE

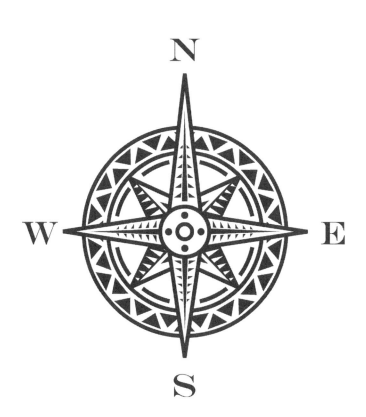

OUR JOURNEY IS OVER

Dear Friends:

Our journey has come to an end. And, as with any trip, there is a part of me that is sad that it is over and a part of me that is happy to return home. As I look back and review all of the places that we have visited, I am amazed at the ground we were able to cover, and yet disappointed because there is still much more that remains to be explored. While this leg of our trip has come to a close, I know that this just opens the door for more adventures. I hope that my itinerary provided you with enough structured events to see what needed to be seen and enough individual time to go where you wanted to go.

Although my job as your guide is over for now, I know that your journey is just beginning and I am filled with excitement over the places you will go, the friendships you will make and the memories you will create. As with any journey, we have marveled at the sights we saw and the scenic backdrop upon which they were placed, but in the end, it was the memories of the people we traveled with that will remain in our hearts and minds the longest. I hope that you will work to keep these relationships alive and vibrant as the passage of time strains against them.

Be sure to send me photos and postcards along the way so that I can live vicariously through your travels. I am interested not only in your destination but the travel process as well. What did you enjoy? What was your greatest challenge? What was the most fun? I really would like to read your travel journals and see your pictures. As your tour guide, I want some help in planning the next trip – you never know when our paths may cross.

Bon voyage!

APPENDIX

A good traveler has no fixed plans, and is not intent on arriving.

Lao Tzu, father of Taoism

APPENDIX CONTENTS

25 DISCUSSION STARTERS

Use the following questions to start a meeting, end a meeting or just as an interesting way to pass time at a leadership retreat. They do not need to be done in any particular order and there are no right or wrong answers.

1. You heard a rumor from just one person that someone is planning on bringing an inappropriate substance on a trip. The person is not a member of your section and is not someone you know very well. How would you handle it if it were:

      a. a Super Soaker squirt gun
      b. tobacco
      c. alcohol

2. You are in rehearsal and you hear someone from another section under his or her breath make a disparaging comment about his or her section leader. To be quite honest, you happen to agree with their comment. What do you do, if anything?

3. You are in the rehearsal room. Your director is not present and a member of the senior class who is also the drum major shares with you their plan to "haze" freshman students at camp. There are rules at your school against hazing. What would you do?

4. You overhear a member of your section tell a member of the color guard that they are the reason your score was so bad at a recent competition. When you approach the member of your section, he points to the score sheets displayed in the director's window and states, "Do the math...it's true!" How do you respond?

5. You have a member of the band who is continually late to rehearsal. You have tried talking to him and it seems to do no good. You volunteered to pick him up but that just makes the both of you late and you soon give up in frustration. What do you do now?

6. Should a senior be put in the top concert group just because they are graduating? What if they are VERY hard-working but are just not that talented? What if they play well enough but there are already too many people in the top group who play that instrument?

7. Do you treat the members of your group equally when it comes to equipment? Do the freshmen get an equal shot at the best uniforms, instruments, lockers, sign-up sheets, etc...? If not, why? Is it justified?

8. How important is talent to your organization? How important is character? Which is more important?

9. You spot a fellow student from your group smoking off campus; would you say anything?

10. You attend a party on a Saturday night and you see members of the student leadership team there drinking. Would you say anything? What if there were younger band members there? What if they were "trash-talking" their director?

11. The night before an honor band audition, a member of your section tells you he is not going to show up to the audition he signed up for because he has not prepared for it. What would you say to him/her? Would you tell your director?

12. Have you ever not given your best effort at rehearsal? If so, how can you justify speaking to your section about giving their best when they have seen you give less than your best?

13. Have you ever broken a group rule and gotten away with it? What would have happened had you been caught?

14. Does your group behave the same in August as it does in November? If not, how does their behavior change? What can you do to combat that?

15. Does your staff play favorites? Is that acceptable? Should people who do more for the group get more benefits?

16. How are the leaders in your group chosen? Is this the best process? How would you improve it?

17. How does the rest of the campus perceive your group? Differentiate between how the band is perceived by the following groups; student council, the football team, cheerleaders and the general student population. If it is not what you want it to be, what can you do to change that? Be specific to each group.

18. What parts of the group have the most staff support? Why? Do you think this is the best use of your resources?

19. What do you see as the greatest strengths of your ensemble? What do you see as the greatest weaknesses? How can you work toward minimizing the impact of your weaknesses?

20. Is there a favorite section in your group?

21. Is there a section that gets ignored?

22. Does the drum line or guard separate themselves from the group? What kinds of things could you put in place to combat that?

23. What is your favorite tradition? What would be a new tradition to start?

24. What are your teacher's best qualities?

25. How can you help your director be more efficient by taking on some tasks for him/her?

50 FUN PIT STOPS ON YOUR JOURNEY

1. Have a section sleepover.
2. Have "themed" rehearsals.
3. Have a prize for section of the week.
4. Have section t-shirts.
5. Email your section a special thoughtful quote every week.
6. Go out to a meal as a section before or after a long rehearsal.
7. Bring them treats for each week with perfect attendance.
8. Make certificates for special accomplishments (learning the opener, etc...).
9. Have a silly sectional bulletin board.
10. Create a section Web site where you can post pictures.
11. Celebrate birthdays.
12. Write individual thank-you notes.
13. Have a scavenger hunt.
14. Go to a concert together.
15. Make a sectional movie.
16. See a motivational movie together (Rocky, Rudy, etc...).
17. Create a sectional tradition.
18. Make posters for other sections.
19. Adopt a band member.
20. Celebrate holidays (Easter Egg Hunts, holiday gift exchange, pumpkin carving contest).
21. Do a community service project for your band, school or community.
22. Make a poster for someone who has worked hard and hang it up anonymously.
23. Make motivating fliers for your section or someone in it and hang them up around the band room.
24. Get a business to donate something small (free scoop of ice cream coupons, for example) and use them as rewards for students in your section.

25. Have a Christmas in July party at band camp.
26. Organize a group of kids to play Christmas carols and go caroling one night. You can also carol to your administrators and the district office.
27. Submit a band announcement for the school marquee.
28. Visit a nursing home together.
29. Find a pen pal section in a band in another state or country and start a message board with them.
30. Post instrument jokes about your instrument. You can find them on the Internet. Read one every day at the start of rehearsal.
31. Run a sectional for the junior high band. Ask the director if he/she would like you to sit in for a rehearsal.
32. Send "Friendship Mail" to each member of your band before a performance. It can be anonymous or signed.
33. Challenge your staff to a game or contest.
34. Challenge another section to a game or contest.
35. Challenge another group on or off campus to a game or contest.
36. Have your sectional in a fountain or some other creative place.
37. Dress in costume for your next rehearsal (superheroes are great).
38. Bring a small grill and grill hot dogs on field before a rehearsal.
39. Invite the local morning show to do a remote from your rehearsal.
40. Have a "dress like your director" day.
41. Have a dance just for your group.
42. Change instruments for twenty minutes while learning drill.
43. Go play for a local pre-school
44. Have a morning radio personality/DJ give a shout out to your group.
45. Write to someone famous, asking them to write back to your section.
46. Put a "Slip and Slide" out during hot rehearsals and use it to cool off.
47. Have a drill down with the staff against students or staff against staff.
48. Do a skit for the whole band once a month.
49. Take a sectional picture in a goofy place and in a goofy way.
50. Your turn – you come up with something and send it to me!

LEADERSHIP TEAM MEETING AGENDA

Date:

Time:

Members present:

Members absent:

Members missing:

Status report on last week's agenda items:

Treasurer's report:

Sponsor report:

Agenda Items:

Motions made:

Motions approved:

Homework assignments:

Next meeting:

Feel free to add or delete items as appropriate. Be sure to post the completed report in several conspicuous places on a consistent basis so the rest of your group knows what is going on.

LEADERSHIP TEAM APPLICATION MEETING

Objective: To help ensure that everyone who applies understands what is expected and how to complete the process in an appropriate manner

Duration: 20-30 minutes

Amount of People: Unlimited

Documents Required: Leadership Application

Brief Instructions: Make the application meeting mandatory for anyone who is planning on applying for a leadership position. Remind students of the demands of the positions and that leadership is a position of service.

Take students through the application process step by step to ensure that they understand what is expected of them. Allow time for questions and discussion. Use the "Leadership Team Application Instructions" document to help guide you through the process.

Spend some time reviewing the job descriptions and what your expectations for that position are. Give them the application deadline and make yourself available for individual questions.

LEADERSHIP TEAM APPLICATION MEETING HANDOUT

Welcome and thank you for showing an interest in being a part of the (_____ _____) Student Leadership Team. We hope you will find the application process to be interesting and enriching regardless of the outcome. This application represents a significant departure from the standard way of selecting student leaders. In addition, some leadership positions have been added or deleted to better fit the current organization. If you have any questions about the process or your application, please do not hesitate to contact (_____) at any time. Good luck, and work hard to best represent yourself through this process.

Your candidacy will be judged on the following criteria:

1. *Past performance*
2. *Quality of your application*
3. *Future leadership potential*
4. *Best fit for the individual and organization*

When completing the application, be thorough, complete, creative, and honest. Don't say what you think your sponsor might want to hear. Say what you really think. Leaders are people who can offer something new and different to the organization. This application process is structured so that you will gain insights into yourself as a person, so please be honest and thorough. You need to open up and show the person who you truly are, or who you aspire to be. Whether you are chosen to participate in the office you apply for is not the penultimate point. Dig deep inside and answer the questions and complete the service project with the intent of learning something new. Please do not fill out this application unless you are prepared to attend the leadership training seminar on (_____). If you have an unavoidable conflict, please see (_____) for a variance prior to submitting your application.

Positions available :   President   Vice-President
                        Morale/Historian   Secretary/Librarian
                        Drum Major   Section Leader
                        Member at Large   Captain

Applications due: All applications must be completed and all elements turned in by (_____). Please be prompt and professional with your application. Some positions will need to participate in interviews and evaluations, which will take place in the afternoon on (_____) after school.

When submitting: Please make sure that all elements are enclosed in one package and are clearly labeled with your name. Any elements of your submission that you would like returned need to be labeled as such. All applications must be typed or done on a word processor. Failure to do so will result in the return of the application to the applicant.

LEADERSHIP TEAM APPLICATION INSTRUCTIONS

The Student Leader Application is designed to:

1. Demonstrate commitment to the program
2. Display student creativity
3. Set a tone for the student leadership team
4. Publicize and recruit for your program
5. Serve as an educational activity, even if the student is not chosen for the position

The successful completion of an application will allow the sponsor to assess the various qualities of each applicant via their written words and actions. The combination of essay questions and service projects should give the sponsor and the student a wealth of opportunities to display their knowledge, commitment, and creativity.

The essay component, which requires the student to interview someone on campus regarding leadership views, will also lend credibility to the process and to your program. Teachers and administrators alike will have a new perspective on the program as they see the process and protocols used in selecting the leadership team. By interviewing fellow colleagues and administrators, students act as ambassadors for the program and learn something about leadership from someone they respect.

Perhaps the greatest benefit in this application is that it is WIN/WIN for the student and the sponsor. By merely applying, students will be forced to examine themselves and assess who they are and what they believe. The program wins because it is the recipient of many service projects and creative activities that will energize and enthuse all the members of the program. In addition, the sponsor will receive a plethora of names to use as a recruiting database for the program.

LEADERSHIP TEAM APPLICATION

Name _____

Position(s) Applying for _____

Current G.P.A. _____   Email Address _____

On a separate piece of paper, please answer the following questions:

1. What are your greatest personal strengths? How will you use them in the position for which you are applying?

2. Interview someone on the campus (student, faculty, or administrator) and ask him or her for views on leadership. What did you learn from your conversation? How is it different from yours?

3. Creating and maintaining an activity is a constant challenge. As a leader, you are responsible for having a direct impact on the quality of the organization. On the attached document, please list the names and phone numbers of people whom you have spoken with that might be interested in joining the organization. THE WORK YOU PUT IN WILL SHOW A GREAT DEAL ABOUT YOUR COMMITMENT TO THE ENTIRE ORGANIZATION.

Complete the following projects:

1. Complete a service project for the (_____) organization. The scope and duration of the project are at your discretion. You may choose something that you think needs to be done, or you may ask the sponsor for a project. If you have any questions about the validity of your chosen project, see (_____) prior to starting it.

2. Open forum: this is where you have the opportunity to show your creative side. You may do anything that you deem appropriate to convince us that you are able to "think outside the box" and address issues in a different manner. This is the portion of the application where you should expect to learn the most about yourself as an individual. Therefore, take a risk here. Once again, this should be fun for you and the organization.

Please understand that, if chosen, you will be held to a higher standard of behavior, performance, and work ethic than your peers. You must be willing to make that sacrifice so that others around you may succeed. Serving in this capacity will not only provide others with a better experience, but will provide you with a tremendous growth opportunity that will serve you for years to come.

Student Signature _____   Parent Signature _____

Scott Lang

For almost a decade, Scott has been educating and entertaining student and adult audiences of all ages through his workshops and keynote presentations. In large and small venues alike, Scott consistently finds creative ways to ensure laughter in learning as he provides attendees the tools necessary to deal with their organizations and their schools. He not only provides an insightful educational presentation but also offers direction on how to implement their newfound knowledge. Scott's workshops are a perfect companion to his keynote presentations and can be customized and/or created to meet any organization's needs.

Scott is also the author of *Leadership Success* (GIA Publications), an interactive DVD/CD-Rom dealing with the development of student leadership. Lang currently resides in Tempe, Arizona, with his beautiful wife, Leah, and their son, Brayden. He can often be found at home changing diapers and sweeping up the tremendous amount of dog hair Samba and Grainger leave behind.

NOTES:

NOTES:

NOTES:

NOTES:

NOTES: